Kid's Chic

Kids' Chic

Great Looks for Kids and How to Put Them Together

Gloria Gilbert Mayer and Mary Ellen McGlone

M. EVANS AND COMPANY, INC.
New York

Library of Congress Cataloging in Publication Data

Mayer, Gloria G.
Kid's chic.

1. Children's clothing. I. McGlone, Mary Ellen.
II. Title.
TT635.M39   1984   646'.36   84-8053

ISBN 0-87131-436-3

M. Evans and Company, Inc.
216 East 49 Street
New York, New York 10017
Design by Lauren Dong
Manufactured in the United States of America
9   8   7   6   5   4   3   2   1

*To Rita London, my sister, who taught me the meaning of
fashion and to her children, Chawn and Derek, who have
provided clothes for my children for many years. And to
Kimmel and Jeffrey, my chic kids.*

Gloria Gilbert Mayer

*To my husband, Sam, and three children, Mike, Molly,
and Michelle, who provide constant, current inspiration
for Kids' Chic and to my mother, who shared with me her
fine taste in clothes.*

Mary Ellen McGlone

Contents

Acknowledgments

This book could not have been completed without the contributions and support of many people. We want to thank the following individuals and corporations (listed in alphabetical order):

American Apparel Manufacturers Association
American Textile Manufacturers Institute, Inc.
Karen Bohnhoff of Dayton's
Jeannie W. Bowers of 5th Avenue of Edina
Pam Busho, Action Hair by Headlines
Kristen M. Carlson of J.C. Penney's
Dayton's Department Store
Sandra Dempsey
Scott Edelstein
Carolyn S. Edwards of the U.S. Department
   of Agriculture
Maureen Heffernan, our editor
Samuel L. Kaplan
Kinney Shoe Corporation
Miriam and Leon Luck, Meredith and Allison
Thomas R. Mayer
The Maytag Company
Evelyn Murray
Katherine Nash
PAR Publishers
Karen Pedro of Donaldson's
Richard Pine, our agent
Mary Lou Rooney of 3M Corporation

JoAnn Rice
Betty Sack
Cindy Schlosser of Dayton's
Ellen Share of Powers
Ginger Shaw
Edie Shepherd of Dayton's
Skyway News
Sara Stern of Ruder, Finn and Rotman, Inc.
Julie Vogel of Main Street Kids
Jan Wondra
The Wool Bureau, Inc.

We want to give special thanks to our illustrators, Sandra Cunningham, Liz B. Dodson, Barbara Gillmor, Steve Parker, and Richard Busby; our photographers, Deb Fritz (principal), Nancy Adler, and Gertrude Gladstone; and our typist, Pat Levin.

In addition, we thank all of the designers and manufacturers that are mentioned throughout this publication who supported this project and contributed both information, photos, and illustrations.

Permissions

The wool symbols used in Chapter 8 were reprinted with permission of The Wool Bureau, Inc., New York, New York.

The Glossary of Textile Terms in Chapter 8 and at the end of the book has been used with the permission of American Textile Manufacturers Institute, Inc.

The chart on textile fibers in Chapter 8 was adapted with permission from *The Person You Are* by Linda Anderson et al., PAR Publishers, Providence, R.I. 1978.

The table in Chapter 10 entitled "Annual Cost of Raising a Child from Birth to Age 18" was adapted from the *U.S. Department of Agriculture Estimates of the Cost of Raising a Child: A Guide to Their Use*, Carolyn S. Edwards, Author. 1981.

The information on stain removal and the Stain Removal Guide in Chapter 14 are reprinted with the permission of The Maytag Company.

The Consumer Care Guide for Apparel in Chapter 14 is reprinted with permission of the American Apparel Manufacturers Association.

Illustrations by:
Sandra Cunningham	Pages 1, 35, 63, 91, 127, 157
Liz B. Dodson	Pages 9, 6–17, 19–23
Barbara Gillmor	Pages 38, 39, 66, 73, 76, 89
Richard Busby	Page 143
Steve Parker	Page 45

About the Authors

Gloria Gilbert Mayer and Mary Ellen McGlone are mothers, wives, working women, and professional writers.

Gloria is a registered nurse, hospital consultant, and professional writer and has been interested in children's fashion as a hobby for many years. Gloria has a doctorate in education from Columbia University and lectures widely on dual-career families, working women, working mothers, and a variety of nursing and health-care issues. Gloria owns and operates a restaurant in St. Paul, Minnesota. She lives with her husband Tom, her daughter Kimmel, and her son Jeffrey in Minnetonka, Minnesota.

Mary Ellen is a fashion expert, lecturer, educator, and fashion columnist for several publications. Mary Ellen's fashion skills include fashion coordinator, producer, and commentator for many large multi-store fashion shows. Mary Ellen is currently employed by a Division of ITT Educational Services and has been involved in all levels of education from primary through post-secondary. Listed in *Who's Who in the Midwest* and *Minnesota's Women's Directory*, Mary Ellen has built a career reputation as an active working wife and mother. She lives with her husband Sam and three children, Michael, Molly, and Michelle, in Minnetonka, Minnesota.

If you would like information about obtaining a detailed, personal wardrobe plan for your child, write to:

Gloria Gilbert Mayer
Mary Ellen McGlone
P.O. Box 1064
Minnetonka, Minnesota 55345-0064

Introduction

Kids' Chic is a practical, thorough, step-by-step guide to dressing, grooming, and buying clothes for your children, no matter what their ages.

Our purpose in *Kids' Chic* is not to tell you what your child *should* wear, but to teach you everything you will need to know to dress your child well, *based on his or her own unique needs, body, and personality.* What is important is to choose a wardrobe that genuinely reflects who your child is and that makes your child look his or her best.

One thing you can be assured of: the kids' fashion industry is paying close attention to the needs of parents and kids. With sales of $6 billion last year, children's wear is currently a boom industry. From the high-status designers such as Dior and Cardin to such favorite kidswear names as Florence Eiseman and Polly Flinders, clothing makers everywhere are rushing out their lines in great excitement to cater to the tastes of you and your kids.

Beginning with Chapter 1, we will introduce you to the Kids' Chic System, explain how it works, and show you how to use it. We have tried to present every aspect of children's clothing, from fabrics, colors, and styles to measuring and sizing your child, from planning wardrobes to developing shopping strategies. We also include a section on today's most active designers and manufacturers: their signature looks and what they do best.

We are also concerned with cost: *chic* does not necessarily mean "expensive." Sections of this book deal not only with wise shopping and bargain hunting, but with determining the *true value* and *true cost* of clothing. Good children's clothing is both timeless and ageless. The price tag alone does not determine the value of a piece of clothing; also important are durability, how often your child wears the item, and the length of time the garment looks good to your child. The Kids' Chic System will show you how to make the most of your clothing dollar.

Kids' Chic will also tell you everything you need to know about the following five basic rules of dressing well:

1. Clothing must be appropriate for your child's age and peer group, as well as for the time, place, and occasion for which it is worn. As your child has no doubt made you aware, his or her peer group has very definite ideas about what's great to wear when and what's not so hot. You should try to take these opinions into account.

2. Clothing should be comfortable, functional, *and* attractive. Don't purchase an item unless it passes all three of these tests.

3. Your child's wardrobe should be as cost-efficient as possible. The best ways to accomplish this are to build a wardrobe primarily of classic styles that stay in fashion, to buy clothing that can be worn three or four seasons a year, and to purchase items that can be worn in a variety of situations. Obtaining a cost-efficient wardrobe does not mean buying clothing with the cheapest price tag.

4. You should choose your child's clothes with his or her individuality, personality, and body in mind. Everyone has her or his own best "look" or "looks," and it takes a good deal of experimentation to find out just what these are. Now is not too soon to start. Once you've figured out the lines and designs that truly flatter your child, the whole project of outfitting that child will become much easier.

5. Good grooming is an essential part of dressing well.

Like anything else, the project of outfitting your children (or yourself for that matter) is what you make it. For some people, it's a thankless task that involves lots of confusing choices and never fails to eat away a large chunk of their take-home pay. For others, it's a fun adventure, an opportunity for experimentation, creativity, and self-expression. Of course, our aim is to show parents and kids how to have fun with clothes. With the help of this book, we hope that moms and dads will be able to develop in their children an early awareness of fashion and a strong sense of what clothes can do. It's never too soon to learn.

Part I

The Basics

1

The Basic Wardrobe: Simple as One, Two, Three

CHILDREN'S FAVORITE STORIES are filled with examples of the importance of clothing. Remember Clark Kent? Kent, the mild-mannered reporter, acquired superhuman power and strength when he traded in his dowdy businessman's clothing for the blue suit and red cape. He even got Lois! And what about Cinderella? For Cinderella, clothing was magic, too. A beautiful ball gown and attendant glass slippers turned the scullery maid into royal material. Voilà! Romance, love, a prince, and a crown!

It's no fairy tale: clothing *can* work magic, no matter what your age. There's no quicker way to feel terrific than to step into an outfit you adore, and that boost will carry you through the day. Great-looking clothes can give your kids the same happy feeling. Of course, happy kids make happy parents!

But with today's hectic life-styles, a simple system for organizing your child's wardrobe is crucial. You do not have the time to spend laboring over starched pinafores or maintaining a closet with one hundred items. What you need is a child's wardrobe *system* as simple as one, two, three.

STEP 1

Pick one color to be the basic color of your child's wardrobe. Believe us, this one rule will do more than any other to simplify your life, organize your kid's wardrobe without your having to think about it, and save you headaches, money, and confusion. In children's wear this can be any color—even black or white. (See Chapter 5 for information on how to select this basic color, and on color in general.) This color can appear in your child's shirts, pants, blouses, skirts, dresses, coats—even in his or her hats and shoes. By building your child's wardrobe around one single color, everything in it will match.

When you think of the alternative, this principle makes sense. A friend recently offered me (Mary Ellen) an elegant Pierre Cardin jacket and skirt in bottle green velvet, which her daughter had grown out of and which she thought my daughter could use. She confessed that it broke both of their hearts to part with it. It was a tradition with this mother to buy a fancy holiday outfit for her little girl, and this one had been purchased only last fall. On their annual shopping excursion, they had seen the dress, had fallen instantly in love with it, and $125 later, were out the door with their prize. Although the suit was magnificent and made the child feel like a princess, the color and, in this case, the fabric limited its use. She wore it exactly three times: Thanksgiving, Christmas, and New Year's Day. But in a more versatile color, combined with slightly less dressy blouses or skirts, the suit could have been a staple in that child's wardrobe. When you love an outfit that much, you don't want to give it away practically brand-new.

Your child should like the basic color you pick for his or her wardrobe, and it should flatter him or her. Any color that fits these two basic guidelines will work for your son or daughter.

Picking a basic color does not mean that every item of your child's wardrobe must be that color, however. It simply means that the wardrobe should be planned *around* that color. For example, suppose your daughter's basic color is blue. Red goes with blue. White, gray, and yellow all go with blue. These colors can be combined either in the same item (a blue-and-red striped blouse, for example) or in different items within one outfit (such as a blue skirt with a white turtleneck).

When combining your child's basic color with another complementary color, the basic color should be more visible than the secondary color. Fifty-fifty combinations are usually not as pleasing to the eye as two-thirds–one-third.

Too many secondary colors in a wardrobe, however, can

make shopping for clothes confusing. If your child's wardrobe includes many different colors, it may also get expensive. So try to find one or two secondary colors to combine often with your child's basic color. (This, too, is discussed in Chapter 5.)

STEP 2

Buy items that are versatile. If you're shopping for a shirt, buy one that can go with several different pairs of pants. (This should be very easy if you are following step one above.) If you're shopping for a sweater, buy one that can be worn two different ways. If you're looking for shoes, buy a pair that can be worn to school, at home, and at formal functions—penny loafers, for example. Buy clothing that can be worn most or all of the year. Children grow so quickly that they usually outgrow items before they wear them out.

Mixing and matching component pieces allows your child to get the most out of the basic wardrobe, while at the same time developing his or her own unique kids' chic style. If you buy versatile, flexible items, you can make your child's wardrobe large and varied at the lowest possible price.

STEP 3

Look for the best quality you can afford. Just because your children are growing doesn't mean you should head straight for the bargain basement. In fact, well-made clothes will often be cheaper in the long run, even though they have higher price tags. Generally speaking, better-made clothing will wear longer, fit better, and look better, even when it is passed down to a second (or even third) child. Of course, the most expensive clothing (particularly items with prestigious designer labels) is not always the best, but in general well-made clothes do cost more.

Below are four sample wardrobe plans: one for a preschool boy, one for a preschool girl, one for a school-age boy, and one for a school-age girl. In designing these wardrobes, we have used only the most basic clothing items; yet each plan allows you to build over twenty different outfits with only fourteen or fifteen pieces of clothing. We find that the number and the mix of items in these plans work well for both parents and kids. The wardrobes are simple and not terribly large, yet they provide a comfortable amount of variety. Your daughter won't become bored to death wearing the same outfit to school every Monday. The wardrobes are full enough to allow you to reach into your child's closet in the morning and pull out an outfit he or she can wear that day. (During one season or another, we've all experienced the headaches of a wardrobe that's too skimpy: running constantly into the laundry room at 7:00 A.M. to fish out a garment worn and washed just days before.) Under any of these plans, your child will get plenty of use out of all her or his clothes, without being forced to wear any one piece so often that it's threadbare by the end of the season.

We invite you to study these four plans and to tailor them to the needs and tastes of your own children.

PRESCHOOL BOY'S WARDROBE ITEMS

Item	Color	Description
	Basic Color: Blue Secondary colors: Red and White	
1. Transitional jacket/ windbreaker	Blue	Basic cardigan style
2. Coat/snowsuit	Red, white, blue	2-piece Snowsuit, jacket can be worn alone except in extreme weather
3. Overalls	Navy and white	Striped denim
4. Overalls/jumpsuit	Powder blue	Short sleeves
5. Pants	Medium blue	Cotton corduroy
6. Pants	Navy	Cotton knit
7. Pants	Navy	Jeans, medium-weight denim
8. Shirt	Red	Polo
9. Shirt	Light blue	Cotton-tailored
10. Shirt	White	Knit, turtleneck
11. Shirt	Navy	Sweat shirt
12. Shirt	Red, white, blue	Plaid
13. Sweater	Red	V-neck pullover
14. Dress outfit	Navy	Sailor suit

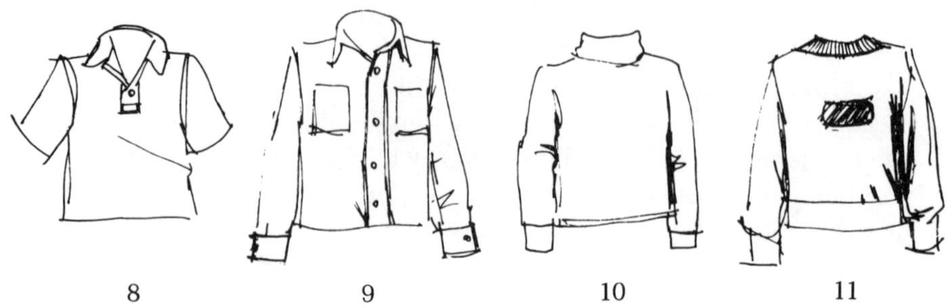

8   9   10   11

PRESCHOOL BOY'S WARDROBE PLAN

Day 1	Day 2	Day 3	Day 4	Day 5
Items: 3, 8	Items: 4, 9	Items: 5, 10, 13	Items: 6, 12, 1	Items: 7, 11
Day 6	Day 7	Day 8	Day 9	Day 10
Items: 3, 11	Items: 7, 8	Items: 6, 9	Items: 4, 11	Items: 5, 10
Day 11	Day 12	Day 13	Day 14	Day 15
Items: 6, 12	Items: 7, 13	Items: 5, 8	Items: 4, 11	Items: 3, 10
Day 16	Day 17	Day 18	Day 19	Day 20
Items: 5, 9	Items: 7, 12	Items: 6, 8	Items: 3, 9	Items: 14

PRESCHOOL GIRL'S WARDROBE PLAN

Day 1	Day 2	Day 3	Day 4	Day 5
Items: 1, 6, 8	Items: 3, 12, 13	Items: 5, 10	Items: 7, 11	Items: 4, 9
Day 6	**Day 7**	**Day 8**	**Day 9**	**Day 10**
Items: 6, 11	Items: 1, 5, 9	Items: 3, 10	Items: 4, 8, 13	Items: 7, 12
Day 11	**Day 12**	**Day 13**	**Day 14**	**Day 15**
Items: 1, 4, 8	Items: 5, 12, 13	Items: 7, 8	Items: 4, 10	Items: 3, 9
Day 16	**Day 17**	**Day 18**	**Day 19**	**Day 20**
Items: 6, 10, 11	Items: 5, 9, 13	Items: 4, 11	Items: 7, 9	Items: 14

PRESCHOOL GIRL'S WARDROBE ITEMS

Item	Color	Description
	Basic Color: Purple Secondary colors: Beige and Tan	
1. Blazer	Beige	Year-round weight
2. Coat/snowsuit	Tan	Quilted, zip-out lining
3. Pants	Tan	Jeans, denim
4. Pants	Lavender	Knit
5. Pants	Caramel	Corduroy
6. Skirt	Lavender tones	Plaid, pleated acrylic
7. Overalls/coveralls	Purple	Polished cotton
8. Shirt	Lavender	Blouse, cotton
9. Shirt	Beige	Polo
10. Shirt	Purple	Sweat shirt
11. Shirt	Lavender tones	Plaid (matches skirt)
12. Shirt	Beige	Turtleneck
13. Sweater	Cream	Cardigan
14. Dress outfit	Tan	Dress

8   9   10

11   12

1
2
3
4
5
6
7
13
14

SCHOOL-AGE BOY'S WARDROBE ITEMS

Item	Color	Description
	Basic Color: Gray Secondary colors: Navy, Red	
1. Jacket	Red, navy, gray	Detachable sleeves for vest, plaid reversible
2. Coat	Navy	Pea jacket
3. Pants	Gray	Chino
4. Pants	Navy	Twill
5. Athletic/jogging pants	Gray with red trim	Fleece
6. Athletic/jogging sweat shirt (matches item 5)	Gray with red trim	Fleece
7. Pants	Gray	Cords
8. Pants	Dark navy	Denim jeans
9. Shirt	White	Button-down oxford cloth
10. Shirt	Red, navy, gray	Plaid
11. Shirt	Gray/blue	Rugby
12. Shirt	Red	Sweat shirt
13. Shirt	Light blue	Turtleneck
14. Sweater	Gray	Ragg wool
15. Sports jacket	Slate blue/gray	Houndstooth

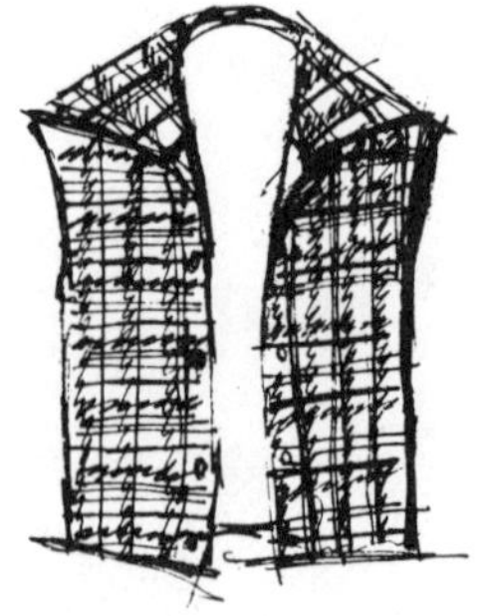

1

2

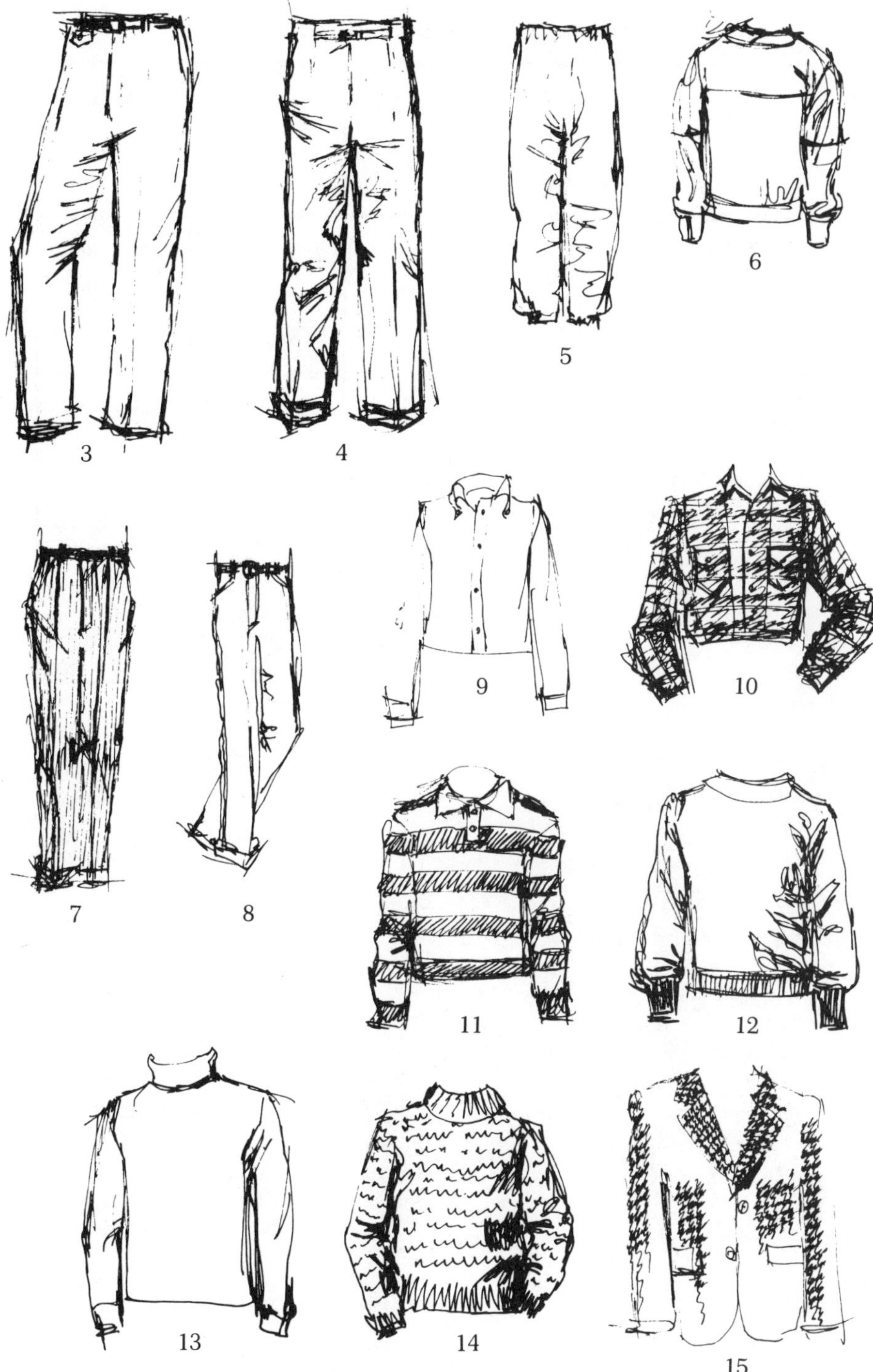

SCHOOL-AGE BOY'S WARDROBE PLAN

Day 1	Day 2	Day 3	Day 4	Day 5
Items: 1, 8, 12	Items: 3, 10	Items: 4, 9, 14	Items: 5, 6	Items: 7, 11
Day 6	Day 7	Day 8	Day 9	Day 10
Items: 8, 13	Items: 7, 9, 14	Items: 3, 13	Items: 5, 12	Items: 4, 13
Day 11	Day 12	Day 13	Day 14	Day 15
Items: 7, 6	Items: 8, 11	Items: 4, 9, 12	Items: 3, 10, 1	Items: 5, 13, 14
Day 16	Day 17	Day 18	Day 19	Day 20
Items: 3, 11	Items: 5, 11	Items: 8, 13, 14	Items: 4, 6	Items: 7, 9, 15

The outfits opposite for Days 1, 5, 6, and 8 show you how you can create a variety of looks by combining versatile pieces. A striped tuxedo shirt adds crispness to the jeans and down jacket worn on Day 1, yet blends easily with the jacket and kilt worn on Day 6. A yellow cardigan tops off a classic skirt and blouse combination on Day 5; the same sweater combined with sweats creates a funky look for Day 8.

SCHOOL-AGE GIRL'S WARDROBE PLAN

Day 1	Day 2	Day 3	Day 4	Day 5
Items: 1, 3, 12	Items: 2, 5, 9	Items: 4, 8, 13	Items: 6, 10	Items: 7, 11, 14
Day 6	**Day 7**	**Day 8**	**Day 9**	**Day 10**
Items: 4, 12, 13	Items: 6, 9	Items: 6, 11, 14	Items: 5, 12, 13	Items: 7, 10, 13
Day 11	**Day 12**	**Day 13**	**Day 14**	**Day 15**
Items: 1, 5, 8	Items: 2, 3	Items: 4, 11,14	Items: 7, 8	Items: 2, 3, 9
Day 16	**Day 17**	**Day 18**	**Day 19**	**Day 20**
Items: 7, 8, 14	Items: 3, 12	Items: 5, 11	Items: 9, 10, 3	Items: 7, 11,13

SCHOOL-AGE GIRL'S WARDROBE ITEMS

Item	Color	Description
	Basic Color: Red Secondary colors: Black, White, and Yellow	
1. Jacket	Red	Down
2. Coat	Gray	Windbreaker
3. Pants	Black	denim jeans
4. Skirt	Red, black, yellow	Plaid, pleated
5. Pants	Gray	Cords
6. Pants	Red	Athletic pull-on
7. Skirt	Black/white	Tweed
8. Shirt	White	Lace trim, long sleeves
9. Shirt	Red	Sweat, kangaroo pocket
10. Shirt	White	Turtleneck
11. Shirt	Yellow	Button-down blouse
12. Shirt	Black/white	Striped tuxedo
13. Jacket	Red	Spencer
14. Sweater	Yellow	Cardigan

2

Life-style Dressing
for Kids

Tₕₑ previous chapter out-
lined basic wardrobe plans, but of course you'll want to adapt
any wardrobe to your child's life-style, personality, and preferences. We've noticed that five major clothing styles seem to
predominate among kids; chances are good that your youngster
already tends toward one of these. The style your child displays
most likely reflects the look and life-style of the family as a whole,
and your children's current style may stay with them all their
lives.

The five fashion life-styles for kids are traditional student,
outdoorsy, preppy, glamorous, and trendy. In the pages that
follow, we list some of the clothing and accessories that are
preferred choices within these styles.

TRADITIONAL STUDENT

Traditional students take practicality and comfort as their
first considerations. Faddish clothes are not part of their wardrobe, and in general, their clothing is without designer labels.
The traditional student look is one of quality and understatement—traditional students always blend in with their environ-
ment. If logos or names are worn, they identify schools, vacation
spots, or personalities. Traditional students would rather die than

18

wear clothes that would make them stand out in a crowd. Classic inconspicuousness is their signature.

Clothing items you may find in the traditional student's wardrobe include the following:

Classic corduroy or twill pants
Basic knee socks
Plaid shirtings
Plain turtlenecks
Classic oxford shirts
Tube socks
Denim dressing
Crewneck and cardigan sweaters
Sweat shirts with school names
No labels showing except names like Lee, Levi's, and Oshkosh
Ski jackets
Clothing by manufacturers who favor traditional styles, such as Carters and DoeSpun

OUTDOORSY

These children favor sportswear. Often athletically inclined, they are able to wear their sweat shirts and jerseys to almost any event—without ever looking out of place. Because they dress for the weather and not according to seasonal fashion trends, their style varies little from year to year. In spring they pull out their T-shirts, and in fall they pull out their flannel shirts. Natural fibers and honest fabrics wear well on these kids.

Clothing items that the outdoorsy kid prefers include the following:

Lumber jackets
Brushed denims—Levi's/
    Laguna/OP
Tennis socks
Football jerseys, baseball
    shirts
Letter sweaters
Kangaroo pocket sweaters
    and jackets

Nike, Puma, Adidas shoes
Flannel shirts
Mountain-climbing shoes,
    Frye boots
Wool socks
Stretch headbands
Athletic pants
Striped sweaters

PREPPY

These kids have their own brand of chic that requires spit-and-polish grooming and rigid attention to small details. It is easy to know if a kid does "preppy" right or wrong. On girls, preppy is a feminine look; on boys it's very masculine. It combines understatement with a little bit of flair.

Preppy clothes include the following:

Argyle socks and sweaters
Alligator labels
Khaki pants
Cuffed pants
Duck shoes and duck boots
Bermuda shorts
Blouses with Peter Pan
    collars
Basic shirtwaist dresses
Metal or tortoiseshell
    headbands
Webbed belts
Circle pins
Cable-knit sweaters
Seersucker

Blue flannel blazers
Sweater vests
Monogramming
L.L. Bean boots
Penny loafers and Sperry
    Top-siders
Madras plaids
Bow ties
Printed cotton turtlenecks
Wrap skirts
Grosgrain ribbons
Pearls
Fair Isle sweaters
Tennis sweaters
Gray flannel pants

GLAMOROUS

In any group of children there are some who positively love to experiment with clothing as fashion. They often follow adult trends as quickly as they are able, and being current is more important than being comfortable. These children love to dress up. They identify themselves by the labels that they wear, and they gain confidence through their fashion experiments. They may pattern their look after favorite celebrities such as Brooke Shields or Princess Diana or local personalities such as sports stars or newscasters. They sometimes have a tendency to overdo, but they like to communicate their sophistication and glamour through their clothes.

Clothing pieces for the glamour kids include the following:

Lace-trimmed socks
Ruffled, trimmed, or sparkle
    socks
Fancy barrettes and ribbons
High-fashion sleeves and
    pronounced shoulders
Wool and silk sport coats
Classic pumps

Outfits by famous designers
    such as Christian Dior,
    Florence Eiseman, Yves
    Saint Laurent and Atanjé
Coordinated warm-up suits
Dresses with ruffles,
    smocking, and pleats
Silk ties for boys
Formal clothes worn on
    everyday occasions

TRENDY

Sometimes children have fun breaking the rules. It's a way to stand out in the crowd. If a child in this category has a trendy item, she or he will enjoy it, even if it's totally out of touch in two years. The trendy style is throwaway chic. It's the opposite of classic and conservative, but it may be fun, express humor, and provide a creative outlet.

Trendy items and styles include the following:

Guess and Complement labels
Flashdance cutup sweat shirts
Exaggerated shoulders
Nontraditional jackets and sweaters
Parachute pants and breaker jackets
Stretch Lycra pants
Animal prints
All kinds of punk and funk looks
Ethnic looks
Army surplus flak jackets
Cutoff, mesh, and tank tops
Pleated pants
Plastic shoes
Cropped pants
Jumpsuits
Pop T-shirts
Satin jackets

DEVELOPING A SENSE OF KIDS' CHIC

How do you do it? Get your child thinking and talking about her or his own style. Analyze it together. Does it fall into one of these categories? Does your child's taste in clothes conform to your own? Who sets your child's standards—mother, father, or an older sibling? Is there somebody famous or somebody at school he or she wants to imitate? Tell your youngster why you dress the way you do and where your own style and taste come from. The more you talk, the easier it will become to select the clothes that will give your child the most pleasure.

There's another sense that must be nurtured if you want to foster in your children a strong sense of style: confidence in their own ability to put clothes together. One mother we interviewed was deliberate and systematic in the way she encouraged that confidence in her daughter from a very early age. "When Sarah was just four years old," Diane recalls, "I set aside one day every week for her to dress herself in whatever clothes she chose. I wouldn't interfere, even if she came down in the morning in a striped blouse, a plaid kilt, knee socks, and sneakers. That was her day. She always looked forward to it." As part of Sarah's early fashion education, Diane also encouraged her to experiment with unisex clothing: denim jeans and vests with rhinestone trim (fashionable then) and miniature hiking boots. "I wanted her to feel comfortable in any kind of look, not just lace, ruffles, and bows," says Diane. These practices paid off. Now fifteen, Sarah has a fashion sense that's strong, sure, and highly individual. No matter how bold the outfit, Sarah can carry it off.

Sarah's mother has also made a point of developing in her children an awareness of the power of clothes to make them feel *special*. Her technique: to take advantage of special events such as weddings, parties, or holidays. For example, a couple of weeks before a family wedding was scheduled to be held, Diane and her son ran across a tuxedo store selling boys' tuxedo shirts for $5.00 apiece. She bought him one with lots of ruffles. As the family planned their outfits for the day, Diane described to Nathaniel the traditional wedding ceremony and the part that formal clothes played in it. "And he had the best time that day!" she remembers. "The shirt made all the difference. It brought him loads of attention from all the relatives—which he of course adored. And because of the shirt, he felt totally involved in the wedding celebration—much more than he would have had he worn a simple blazer."

These are only a few of the many ways to stimulate children's interest in clothes and fashion. But we notice two ingredients in Diane's approach that guarantee success, and we'd like to pass them along. First, we notice that she really pays attention to clothes. This interest goes beyond just keeping up with the fashion magazines. Diane feels that outfitting herself and her family is an important pursuit that requires energy and thought to do well. Realizing this, she's willing to devote the effort needed. Second, her approach to dressing is obviously a creative one. As her examples illustrate, a little creativity can go a long way in providing kids the chance to have fun with clothes at very low cost.

3

Beyond the Basics

FASHION TERMS

To use the Kids' Chic System properly, you should know the meanings of a few basic terms. Understanding these terms will also help you to understand the world of fashion (including children's fashion) in general.

Fashion is the general acceptance of certain kinds of clothing during a particular time. This acceptance is a reflection of contemporary values and attitudes, which change constantly. Fashion is also determined by place as well as by time. What is accepted as fashion in London or Hong Kong may not be considered fashionable in Atlanta or Cheyenne, Wyoming. The cowboy hat that was a must out West may only sit in the closet in an East Coast home.

Likewise, fashion varies among different groups of people. Younger children are quite proud to wear clothing emblazoned with their favorite superhero or Sesame Street characters, but many school-age children may be embarrassed to wear such items.

Since jeans have become an accepted general item of clothing to wear to school (and to other places that once shunned jeans, and any pants, on girls), we can say that jeans are currently *in fashion.*

While fashion changes gradually over years, individual *styles* are shifting constantly. Although the words *fashion* and *style* are often used interchangeably, each has its own distinct meaning.

A *style* of clothing is an item with distinctive features that make it unique and different from other similar items of the same type. For example, the current *style* calls for jeans that are tailored and either straight-legged or slightly baggy. Stitching on jeans pockets is also currently *in style*.

The individual variation within a certain style is called *design*. The specific pattern of stitching on the pockets of a particular brand of jeans is part of that brand's *design*.

A fashion *trend* is the direction in which fashion is moving. A *trend* is made up of a series of new and changing *styles* and reflects a gradual *change in style*. In women's clothing, it usually takes about seven years from the time a trend begins, through the time it becomes the status quo, to the time when a new trend begins to take its place. Men's trends usually last close to ten years. Children's fashion trends fall somewhere in the middle.

In contrast, a *fad* is a style that has a sudden sweep of popularity, a quick decline, and a short life overall. Fads rarely last longer than a year or two, and sometimes much less. The Flashdance look, the Little Orphan Annie look, and Cabbage Patch and E.T. clothes were all fads. Initially, leg warmers appeared to be a fad, but because they serve a useful purpose, they may not die out. As they have stayed around, they are a fashion trend and may become a classic.

Three other terms that are commonly used in fashion are *high fashion*, *mass fashion*, and *classic*.

High-fashion styles are those created by the big-name clothing designers. Magazines such as *Vogue* are primarily devoted to *high fashion*. High-fashion clothes are usually very expensive, and because of extremely sophisticated styling, they may be difficult for many people to wear. High-fashion styles therefore have limited acceptance and appeal—except, of course, among rich and fashionable people. Designers like Bill Blass, Yves Saint Laurent, and Calvin Klein design high-fashion clothing, for the most part.

On the other hand, *mass fashions* are the styles and designs that are accepted and worn by a great many people—polo shirts, for example, or jogging suits.

Classic fashions are the styles, designs, and clothing items that have been in style *and* in fashion for a long time and that will continue to stay in style and in fashion indefinitely. Girls' kilt skirts and boys' button-down dress shirts are two examples of *classic fashion.*

FOUR CHIC POINTS

Any kid who wants to be chic must take into account the four general principles of kids' chic: style, appropriateness, individuality, and grooming. We'll go through these four points one by one.

STYLE. As we emphasized at the beginning of this book, dressing well doesn't mean simply wearing what is currently in style. What is attractive on one person may look awkward, silly, or even ugly on another, even if it is absolutely up-to-the-minute. So do not blindly follow the trends. This does not mean that you shouldn't keep abreast of current children's fashion. You do for adult fashions, so do the same for your kids. Children's styles do date, and quickly. Not paying attention can lead to costly mistakes.

The key to dressing your son or daughter stylishly is to buy *well-made classic clothing that stays in style year in and year out.* Although these pieces may not have the lowest price tags, they really pay off in the long run in appearance, durability, and value. This is especially true if you can pass the clothes on to a younger child, but it is also true if you have one child. Although many people avoid expensive and moderately priced clothes for children because kids seem to outgrow them so quickly, cheap items look cheap, wear out fast, and are almost never as comfortable as well-made clothes. *Quality clothes have a quality look.*

APPROPRIATENESS. No matter what the occasion is, your child can and should be well dressed for it. This means that you should pay as much attention to the clothes your daughter plays in as you do to what she wears to school and church. Playclothes are what kids wear 80 percent of their childhood years. One good rule to keep in mind is to always purchase clothes to fit the occasion: *don't* try to force your child to act according to his or her clothes. One mother bought her child nothing but ex-

Striped cotton sweaters over pull-on pants, all from Merona Sport, are classic choices for boys and girls. (Photo: Merona Sport)

pensive and dressy pants and then refused to allow him to play kickball because he might get those pants dirty. This is unreasonable and unfair. Instead, the mother should have also bought him jeans for sports and roughhousing.

Appropriateness also refers to the makeup of your child's entire wardrobe. The kinds of clothes you buy should fit the kinds of activities that keep your child busy. Don't buy your nine-year-old Little Leaguer a wide array of expensive and beautiful Brooks Brothers shirts that can only be worn on fairly formal occasions. There aren't going to be that many formal occasions for him to wear them to. Each item of clothing, and your child's wardrobe in general, should fit his or her activities and life-style.

INDIVIDUALITY. Be sure to consider carefully your child's height, weight, build, personality, and size for her or his age when purchasing an item of clothing for your child and when planning her or his overall wardrobe. The clothes your child wears should emphasize his or her best features (good posture, luxuriant hair) while camouflaging those features that are not flattering (chubbiness or an extra-long neck).

If your child's body is close to the norm for his or her age, then selecting styles that flatter his or her proportions should be fairly easy. However, if your child is difficult to fit because of height, weight, or proportions, then proper fit becomes the single most important factor in choosing clothes. Nevertheless, it is necessary that you consider his or her body and proportions objectively and learn what looks best on your child. Don't fool yourself into pretending that a fat child is "a little chubby" or that your five-foot-tall third grader is "a little big for his age." Look at your child realistically.

The best way (and in many cases the only way) you can tell whether or not an article of clothing will work is to have your son or daughter try it on. There is no substitute for having your child try something on in front of a mirror, and having him or her move, stretch, and even sit in the clothes. Use your judgment and your intuition.

Judgment and individuality also mean purchasing clothing for your children that they like to wear. Never purchase an article of clothing that your children don't like; either they won't wear it, or they'll wear it, hate it, and be angry or grumpy because of it. We know of lots of parents who have indirectly caused quarrels and fights because they forced their children to wear clothes they didn't want to wear. (Of course, you should not allow your child to wear jeans to a funeral. But, for example, when you are purchasing a blazer or dress slacks for him, you should be sure to buy items he feels comfortable and happy in.) Instead of using forcefulness, teach your kids the principles of kids' chic for themselves, so they can be more independent in choosing their own clothes. Remember, a garment must both *look good and feel good*. Don't buy anything that looks great on your child but feels scratchy, tight, or uncomfortable. If it's uncomfortable, your child won't want to wear it.

The touchiest aspect of individuality is dealing with gifts. Scott, the son of a friend, was mailed a perfectly hideous shirt for his birthday by his grandparents. When the grandparents came to visit a few months later, they asked Scott to wear the shirt when they all went out to dinner. Obviously, neither Scott nor his parents wanted him to wear the shirt. He did wear it, but he was very embarrassed.

If your child is given an article of clothing that you both simply hate, you should try to exchange it if possible. Sometimes you can politely ask the person who gave the gift to exchange it. For example, "Would you mind very much if we asked you to exchange the sweater you gave Jeanette for something in blue? She looks so good in blue and she already has more than she needs in polka dots." Of course, if a piece of clothing is the wrong size, you should have no qualms at all about asking the person who gave the gift to exchange it for something in the right size. (In fact, the giver may be insulted if you do *not* ask to exchange it.) You might be able tactfully to suggest a different design or color at the same time.

If you are fairly sure that the giver will not take kindly to exchanging the item for a different design or color, then put that garment in your child's closet and let it hang there, unworn. Don't make your son or daughter wear it, except occasionally in the presence of the person who gave him or her the gift. This should be viewed as a necessary evil, and it is the *only* time when you should ever insist that your child wear something he or she does not like. After six months or a year, your child will have grown out of the garment, and you can give it away.

If, by some chance, you are the giver of a gift of clothing to a child, and that gift never gets worn, do not take it personally. You're not alone. Instead, buy a gift other than clothing next time—or, if you prefer, buy a gift certificate to a good clothing store.

GROOMING. Dressing well also includes good grooming. The endless battle over grooming habits goes on in every family household we know. It involves daily interrogation sessions: "Did you brush your teeth?" "Don't go out that door until you've combed your hair!" "When was the last time you took a bath?" For some reason, many kids love to resist practicing these habits. Don't let their resistance wear you down. A clean, well-groomed kid is a cute kid. Dirt and mess aren't chic. In Chapter 15, we'll give you advice on the best ways to handle the issue of grooming with your children.

MATTERS OF TASTE

Kids have many different reasons for wanting or not wanting certain clothes, and some reasons have nothing to do with how an item actually looks on them. Of course, your child is likely

Seeing is believing. The good looks of this bright-eyed young-ster make a convincing case for good grooming habits.

to want clothing that is flattering, but several other factors are equally important to children and young adults. We'll go over each of these factors briefly.

CONFORMITY. Most children and young adults are strongly influenced by peer pressure. They like to have the labels, brand names, styles, and designs that everyone else has, and they may feel left out if their clothes do not match those of their friends. Their sense of need is related more to what clothes others have (or don't have) than to what they genuinely need. You'll see signs of this quite often—probably every time the question of clothes comes up. Don't let this worry or anger you; it's normal for children to want to conform. On the other hand, trying to explain to your child that this need to conform is illogical or silly probably won't work. The need is there. Your child feels it is very real, and therefore it is very real. Rather than ignoring your children's concern about fitting in, or trying to talk them out of it, try to purchase clothing that meets this need while at the same time giving them their own particular kind of chic.

Remember, looking chic doesn't necessarily mean dressing utterly unlike everybody else. In fact, generally the opposite is true: for a child to be chic, he or she will normally wear some variation of the currently accepted styles and designs. There are plenty of easy ways to stay informed about these. Look at department store catalogs. Take note of children's wear ads in magazines. Take a look around when you attend school functions, and observe what the best-dressed kids are wearing. Encourage your child to talk about the clothes and extras that are in vogue with classmates. Go window-shopping with your child.

The need to conform, along with a general caution and fear of disapproval, is strongest and most common among children between the ages of eight and fourteen. During these years, children are quite self-conscious, and they sometimes want to be as inconspicuous as possible. If your child's desire to follow the crowd seems silly or unreasonable to you, remember that we adults have exactly the same need. If you're planning your outfit for a business meeting or formal dinner, you'll certainly take time to ponder what others will be wearing. The truth is that adults need to stick to convention just as much as children do. The difference, however, is that the conventions of children's clothing change more quickly and more often than do adult styles, and children are much more susceptible to clothing fads.

Although most children feel a strong need to conform to their peers' style of dress, don't wonder or worry if your child is free of it. If your son or daughter prefers clothes that are different from what most other kids are wearing, but that are attractive and still basically in fashion, wonderful! Don't go overboard and try to get your child to conform to current fads and styles *more* than he or she would like. We have a friend Mark, now an adult, whose parents always wanted him to wear the latest styles because "they're all wearing it." As a result he deliberately avoided clothes that were currently in style. Today he still avoids trends in style and isn't comfortable shopping for his own clothing.

THE NEED FOR RECOGNITION. The desire for recognition and approval also affects the way children look at clothing. Children, like adults, take pleasure in the admiration they receive for something they are wearing. All kids want clothes that simply fit in, but most will also want a few outfits or pieces that will draw attention.

Kids can get carried away sometimes. If baggy jeans are popular, your son may want to have the baggiest in the school. Your daughter may want a pair of earrings that are very eye-catching, or she may want to wear three or four pairs simultaneously. Or, if bright pink is a popular color, she may want to wear nothing but pink: pink shoes, pink socks, and pink hats. If your son or daughter goes off on a kick, we think it's fine to indulge him or her—to a point. Kicks seldom last long. Once they're over, you and your child can steer back to your everyday chic.

REBELLION. This is the opposite of conformity: it means dressing against a current or widely accepted style. Some older children in particular want to be different, just as badly as other children their age want to dress exactly like everyone else. Punk styles began in just this way.

Sometimes rebellion is actually a form of conformity. Often a child will want to rebel in exactly the same way her or his friends are rebelling. Rebellion, hard as it may be for you to take, is usually a very healthy sign of your child's emotional growth, provided it is expressed in something as harmless as taste in clothing. For most youngsters, it's a stage that normally lasts between six months and two or three years.

IMPULSE AND DETAIL. Children often are attracted to clothes on sheer impulse, more strongly and more often than are adults. We find that our kids have a tendency to look at one detail rather than at the larger whole. For example, a child (especially a young child) may beg for a shirt because she likes its color or because of the design on the back, even though the shirt doesn't fit or is made of an uncomfortable fabric. Or your son may want a pair of red Bermuda shorts that does indeed look great on him but doesn't fit with anything else in his wardrobe. In such a case, we think you're better off if you simply explain to your son why you can't buy the shorts.

Sometimes, for no apparent reason, your child may dislike a terrific piece of clothing and will refuse to wear it if you buy it. If this is the case, pass it by. Don't buy an item for your child unless both you and your child like the way it looks, fits, and feels. This may seem like an impossible task at first, but it's not. Remember that you won't be wearing the garment; your child will. So take his or her tastes and desires seriously, and don't push yours too hard unless something is simply very wrong for your child.

Part II
Looking Good

4

Reading Between the Lines: Line, Design, and Style

S O THERE YOU ARE, WITH ONE or more kids to dress and an endless array of pint-sized outfits to choose from. What criteria can you use to match the clothes to the kid? We suggest you start by reading between the lines. Focus on the lines of a piece of clothing, on the skeletal structure of its design. The lines and design of an item of clothing can create optical and psychological illusions that flatter your youngster's body, enhance proportions, and improve appearance. If a garment is poorly designed or if its lines are not appropriate for your child, it's sure to defeat the purpose. At the very least, that garment can turn attention away from the child's best features. At worst, it will make him or her look awkward or unattractive. For great-looking kids, you have to go back to the lines and designs that help them look their best.

A clothing designer can work magic by building optical illusions into her or his garment. A designer can pull one's eye in virtually any direction by placing dominant lines in the most flattering position. If a garment has strong vertical lines, the illusion of height and slenderness results. Width is added by horizontal lines. Diagonal lines draw the eye up and across, creating the illusion of greater height and width. Sharp, angular lines point out the surrounding area, while curved lines soften the shape and outline of that area. The direction of a curve is important. Downward curves sometimes appear droopy, while upward curves softly add life.

The clothes that do the most for your child are the ones that make his or her body look well proportioned. *Proportion* is defined as the relationship of the parts to the whole. When a child looks well proportioned, each part of his or her body seems the right shape and size in relation to the rest of the body. If your child is wide, round, or narrow in unexpected places, the proper clothing can help.

In order to be able to choose clothing with flattering lines and designs, you first need to be aware of your child's measurements and proportions. Measure your child's chest, waist, leg inseam, and hips. Take note of how each of these compares with the ideal proportions for your child's size. What is his or her basic body structure? Is your child thin? Heavy? Short? Tall? Does he have a long or short neck? Is his torso long or short? Are his arms and legs lanky or short and thick? Does he have a defined waist? If you look at his shoulders from the front, back, and side, what do you see? Are they even or slumped, narrow or broad?

It is also a good idea to look at the shape of your child's face. This also influences the lines in clothing that should be selected. For example, Jennifer has a very square-shaped face. At age nine, her body is somewhat barrel-shaped—not really chubby,

Strong horizontals and verticals create balance in this young skier's outfit from J.C. Penney. The wide bands of color in the parka are countered by the vertical lines of the ski pants, which give the leg added length. (Photo: J.C. Penney)

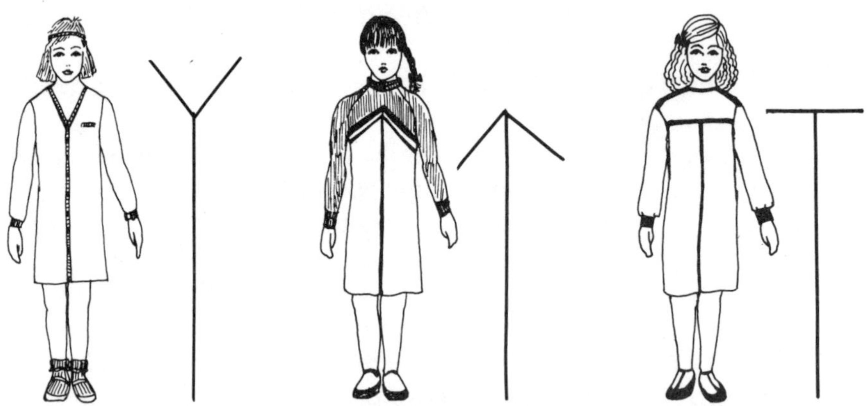

Note the effects created above in several dresses by the placement of dominant lines. Below, stripes make your child look wide or narrow, depending on their direction.

but with no defined waist. Her grandmother from Scotland sent her a plaid dress with a square neckline, a combination that only served to accentuate the squareness of her face and body. To compensate, Jennifer's mother added an oversize white bertha collar to the dress. This alteration, which covered up the square neckline and drew the eye away from the girl's waist, made the dress work beautifully.

TIPS FOR DRESSING A THIN CHILD

- Horizontal lines can soften your child's appearance and make her or him look wider.

- Multiple lines or bands of color in any direction widen a narrow figure and shorten a tall one.
- Outfits and individual pieces made up of contrasting colors or patterns will make a child appear heavier and shorter.
- Shirts, blouses, and dresses with yokes of a different color will make her or his shoulders appear broader.
- Plaids make your child look both broader and taller. So do diagonal lines.
- The curved lines of ruffles, scallops, or drapes soften edges and expand proportions.
- Belts and sweaters are good accessories for a thin child.
- Textured fabrics such as corduroy and tweed will add bulk to your youngster's appearance.
- Dressing your child in layers can help her or him look heavier. In the winter, for example, a thin girl might wear a turtleneck under her blouse and a blazer over it. Double layers of shirting are a solution that's particularly fashionable today.
- Bulky items such as sweat suits and sports jackets help beef up a thin child's appearance.

TIPS FOR DRESSING A HEAVY CHILD

- Straight vertical stripes will add height and slimness.
- Accents at the ends of lines (cuffs on pants, different-colored necklines and collars, for example) will make a child appear taller and slimmer.
- Smooth fabrics without shiny finishes look best on heavy children.
- Make sure that the horizontal lines in a garment don't cut across the child's body at its broadest point.
- The placement of a belt can dramatically alter the appearance of a heavy child's proportions. The farther away the belt is from the center of the body, the taller and slimmer he is likely to appear.
- Scarves, ties (except bow ties), cravats, and so on help thin out a heavy child's appearance.
- Logos or appliqués near the shoulder or on the sleeves carry the eye away from the center of the body.

Plaids and ruffles in the blouse and soft, full lines in the trousers work to expand a thin child's proportions. Up-and-down lines make a chubby child look taller and slimmer.

- Vertical rows of buttons or snaps make a heavy child look taller and thinner.
- Outfits based around a single color are the best choice for heavy children because they make them look taller and thinner.
- Pants with crisply pressed seams are slimming.

In general, lines that make a child look thinner also make him or her look taller, and lines that make a child appear heavier also make him or her appear somewhat shorter. Small children can look taller in "heavy child" clothing; tall children can look smaller when they wear "thin child" clothing.

Dressing a child who is tall *and* heavy, or one who is thin *and* small can present special problems. Deal with your child's slenderness or heaviness first. Try out some of the techniques listed above. Some of them will add to or thin out your child without altering his or her apparent height. Plaids and diagonal lines are also useful in making a thin child appear both taller and heavier. Go ahead and experiment.

Remember, too, that proportion is the key. Children who are short or tall for their age can still look just fine if they appear properly proportioned. But a child who looks too thin or too heavy starts out with a disadvantage. So focus first on width rather than height.

5

Color Me Chic

IN CHAPTER 1, WE RECOMMEND-
ed that you plan a wardrobe around one color, so it's worth your
while to find the colors that flatter your child the most. When
shopping for their youngsters, parents all too often select clothing in colors that they themselves prefer or that they consider
"in good taste"—which usually means conservative tones. After
they've narrowed their choices down that far, and especially
when picking out a pair of trousers or a skirt, they apply the
real acid test: "Will it show the dirt?" At the end of this process
of elimination, the child can easily wind up with lots of basic
pieces of brown, tan, navy, gray, black, and blue-jean blue.

But children love colors, bright colors, and bright, bold colors
abound in children's clothing. What's more: kids look wonderful
in colorful clothes. You may not look so great in banana yellow
pants, but your six-year-old can carry it off. If you want your
kids to look chic, you have to take advantage of what color can
do for them.

The three basic factors that determine what colors look best
on a child are eye color, hair color, and skin tone. While most
people can wear virtually any color, the shades, tints, and in-
tensities of each are what determine how flattering a particular
color is on your child.

Before we go on, let's define some basic color terms.

Shade of color refers to its darkness—how much black or gray, if any, is added to that basic color to darken it. Navy blue is a deeply shaded blue.

Tint is the opposite of shade. It refers to the amount of white added to a color to make it lighter. Pink is a tint of red.

Intensity is a measure of a color's brightness. The same color can be more intense in one pair of pants than in another because of the fabric, finish, or dye used.

Hue and *tone* are synonyms for *color*, and most fashion books use the three words interchangeably.

Primary colors are the three basic colors: red, blue, and yellow.

Secondary colors are those colors that are formed by combining two primary colors. Secondary colors are orange, green, and purple.

Tertiary colors are created by combining primary colors with one or more secondary colors. Aqua and chartreuse are tertiary colors.

COLOR SELECTION

Since everybody has his or her own unique combination of hair color, eye color, and skin tone, everyone also has his or her own particular group of flattering colors, shades, and tints. To find the best and most flattering colors for your child, you should do some color testing. This should be done in natural sunlight and is a simple and fairly quick process. The first step is to discover your child's color preferences. This works best with children over four years old. You can also try this part of the test on younger children, but very young kids may still have a simplistic and underdeveloped sense of color, so you may not want to treat the results too seriously. A child of three may only like red, for example, or only red and blue because Superman wears those colors.

Put together an assortment of color swatches. You can use pieces of fabric, colored paper, paint chips, or actual garments for the test. Show them to your child one at a time. Ask your child how much he or she likes each color as you show it. If you are holding up items of clothing, make sure your child understands that he or she is to respond only to the color of that item, not to its style or any other facet of its appearance. Write down what he or she says about each color.

Once you know your child's preferences, you can look at what colors and shades seem to be the most flattering. Focus on the face, eyes, and hair. Consider the various colors, one by one, by holding them next to your child's face. See which are most flattering to his or her skin tone, hair, and eyes, in that order. Pay attention primarily to your child's face, not to the color itself. Having your child stand in front of a white, beige, or tan background works best. Allow enough time for each color so that you can get a clear feeling for its effect. Write down which colors look most flattering to your child, which look somewhat flattering, and which do not look flattering at all.

Remember that proper color selection enhances your child's face and body. A color that is too intense or too weak is not flattering; the wrong color can make a child's complexion look blotchy, pale, or sallow.

Don't expect to identify all your child's best colors in one round of testing. Your child probably won't have the patience for a long analysis. And as you get better at color analysis (and you will as the time goes by), you will get more and more of an idea of what colors look best. The colors that your child prefers

Eye color, hair color, and complexion determine the colors that will look best on your child.

and that look great on her or him should be the basic colors in your child's wardrobe. Other colors that can appear occasionally in the wardrobe can be ones that look good on your child and that he or she at least did not dislike and colors that your child liked and that looked at least passably good to you.

Below is a list of the six primary and secondary colors and their general attributes and affects on others. Remember, these attributes are generalities only. Although knowing these attributes is useful in selecting colors and clothing, your most important considerations are the results of the color test described above.

IMPACT OF COLOR

Color	Psychological Cues
Primary colors (appealing to young children)	
Red	Warm and aggressive; associated with fire, blood, excitement, and danger.
Blue	Cool and restful; associated with water, honesty, peace, and serenity. Blue has a masculine feeling but is a basic wardrobe color for children of both sexes.
Yellow	Warmly appealing and bright; associated with youth, cheerfulness, and open space.
Secondary Colors (formed by combining two primary colors)	
Orange	Earthy, warm, harvest color; associated with autumn, wealth, and a feeling of plenty.
Green	A quiet, restful color of nature; associated with new life, growing grass, summer, and youth.
Purple	A rich, warm, elegant color; associated with royalty, elegance, and creativity.

COLOR COMBINING

By properly combining colors in your child's outfits and wardrobe, you create harmonious images. Careful color combining also makes a wardrobe easier to manage and coordinate.

Three of the most popular and successful color combinations are *monochromatic combinations, complementary combina-*

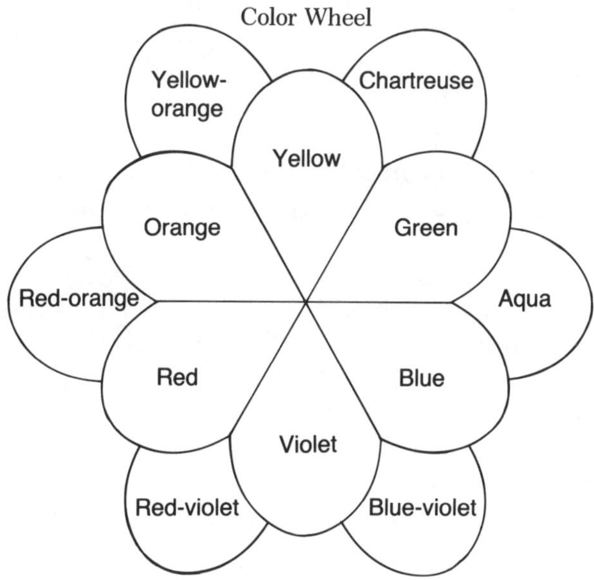

tions, and *adjacent color combinations.* To get some idea of the relationships between colors, see the standard color wheel above.

A *monochromatic* outfit is made up of items that are all the same basic color but that use two or more different tints or shades of color. For example, a boy who looks good in brown might wear dark brown shoes and socks, light brown corduroy pants, and a medium brown pullover shirt. By adding white or black to the basic color, you have created variety, and each item has its own distinct appearance, which is at the same time in harmony with all the other items in the outfit. A monochromatic outfit does not have to be an all-body paint job where every item is exactly the same color, shade, and tint. For small children these color plans are effective.

A *complementary* combination is made up of colors that are located *opposite* each other on the color wheel. Yellow and purple are complementary colors; so are blue and orange, and red and green. When complementary colors are used together in an outfit, they should not be of equal intensity. An ideal complementary combination would include one pure color and one tinted or shaded color. An attractive complementary outfit might include a blue skirt (pure color) and a peach blouse (a tint of orange) plus blue shoes.

An *adjacent* color combination combines two colors that are next to each other on the color wheel. Adjacent colors include blue and green, yellow and orange, red and purple, green and yellow, and so on. These colors are often combined together in prints, plaids, stripes, and other patterns. A girl's good-looking outfit made up of adjacent colors might include a blue-and-green plaid flannel shirt, blue slacks, dark blue shoes, and a dark green scarf.

Every child has his or her own color personality, and the colors in each wardrobe should harmonize with that personality. However, children can be divided into four basic color groups, or "teams" as we prefer to call them. Color selection and shopping can sometimes be easier if you know which team your child belongs to. We call the four teams Cardinals, Bluejays, Eagles, and Orioles.

Cardinals' characteristics include the following: They may have very white or very dark skin. Asian and Mediterranean children with golden or olive skin tones fit this category; so do all black children except for those with very light skin. Cardinals' complexions can sometimes have a rosy or pink undertone, but their complexions are not ruddy.

Cardinals wear clear, distinct, and vivid colors, as well as bright contrasts. Primary colors look stunning on them. Gary Coleman is an example of a Cardinal.

Eagles have peachy, golden, or coppery skin. Usually (but not always) their hair has reddish hues, hints, and highlights. Some light-skinned black children are Eagles. Drew Barrymore is an Eagle.

Eagles look best in neutral colors, beige tones, and whites. Warm earth tones and muted colors are particularly flattering to these children, although some brighter colors next to the face can lighten and brighten the effect.

Bluejays frequently have very pink or very light beige complexions. They may have freckles, and their hair is usually in the blond to brown range. Amy Carter is a typical Bluejay.

Bluejays look best in softer colors. Pastels and soft whites seem to flatter these children, but darker tones of plum, maroon, and gray blue also enhance their looks. Muted tones work better than pure, intense colors.

Here, a light shirt and a dark shirt create different effects in one boy's appearance.

Orioles have rosy cheeks. They have peach, ivory, or beige complexions with a golden undertone. Their hair is usually golden blond, strawberry, honey, auburn, or golden brown. Orioles' colors are delicate, clear, creamy, and fresh. They are not harsh or extreme, but tend to stay light and clear. An Oriole looks better in a peach than in an orange, and in a buff instead of a white. Turquoise and periwinkle are better than powder blue or navy, since too much color can overpower Orioles' fair complexions. Ricky Schroeder is a good example of an Oriole.

6

Accessories for Fun

REAL CHIC—FOR ADULTS AS WELL as for kids—comes from the artful, knowing use of accessories. When you've built a wardrobe from classic pieces—as we've recommended in this book—this is doubly true. The clothes you buy will be both timeless and probably pretty basic-looking, but the right accessories can bring your child's look up-to-the-minute and make it personal and memorable.

The other great thing about accessorizing—especially when it comes to buying for kids—is that it's somehow a less *serious* part of outfitting a child. If you're contemplating buying a good winter coat or a blazer, you'll certainly be very deliberate and careful in making your decision. But when it comes to buying some multicolored shoelaces, socks decorated with hearts, or a bright red pair of suspenders, you can indulge your children's whims and sense of fun and fantasy.

In this chapter, we give you some pointers on the features to look for when shopping for accessories and how to use them to best effect. Do consider one thing: children do not wear accessories as easily or as discreetly as adults. Overdressing children with accessories is a more common problem than underdressing. Young children, especially, love to wear many or all of their accessories at once.

Laurie, the six-year-old daughter of one of our neighbors, loves to experiment with clothes and has certain favorite acces-

sories. Laurie's mother, Eve, has tried to teach her how to use them properly. But every time they get ready to go out, Laurie seems to add half of her accessories to her outfit. Eve finally sat down with her daughter and discovered the reason why: anything Laurie has ever been complimented on she tries to include in every outfit.

THE M & M POINT SYSTEM

The M & M (Mayer and McGlone) Point System is a good way for both you and your child to determine how many accessories to use with any outfit. The Point System gives you rough guidelines to help simplify dressing and to help children avoid a gaudy appearance.

Here's how the Point System works:

1. Let your child choose the outfit he or she wants to wear, complete with any accessories he or she desires. Then give that outfit a certain number of points, based on the following scale:

2. Give your child *1 point* for *every* item in the outfit that is visible—shirt, blouse, skirt, jacket, turtleneck, sweater, jumper, coat, tie, dress, bracelet, necklace, ring, purse, eyeglasses, watch, hat, scarf, and so on. Shoes and boots

receive 1 point for the pair; so do sandals and flip-flops. *Visible* socks, nylons, or tights each receive 1 point per pair. A pair of earrings receives 1 point.

3. *Add 1 additional point* for each of the following items: bright stripes; any embroidery or decoration; flowers; any patterned, plaid, or print garment; any fancy hairstyle, and any hair ornamentation (headbands, flowers, ribbons, fancy barrettes).

4. In general, a child will be well dressed if his or her outfit has between 6 and 9 points. Fewer points means the youngster is probably underdressed; more points means he or she is very likely overdressed. This applies equally to boys and girls of all ages.

SHOES

Children's feet are special. They demand care—because ultimately they will be responsible for more than hopscotch and jump rope. Good posture, grace of movement, and athletic ability depend on healthy development of the feet. From a child's first faltering step to that triumphant kick for a soccer goal, children's feet are meant for action. Children's shoes must enhance movement, not restrict it.

Children's feet are not miniature versions of adult feet. They require careful attention to ensure healthy growth and development. Because the bones in children's feet are malleable and soft, it is extremely important to fit their shoes correctly. Improperly fitted shoes can cause permanent damage. So take your children's shoes and feet seriously. When shopping for children's shoes, you should be concerned with fit, comfort, quality, and value.

INFANTS. Architects tell us that if building foundations were as inadequately proportioned as feet are to the rest of the body, skyscrapers would topple. An infant's feet are only about three inches long, and yet, ultimately, they become the foundation of a long walking career.

The bones (all twenty-six of them) of these small feet are extremely malleable and soft. Doctors recommend that infant's feet, because they are so pliant, be totally unencumbered so infants can wiggle their toes freely. Even the slightest binding could cause damage. Here are a few pointers to remember:

- Use foot coverings for warmth only; make sure that booties are roomy.
- Check pajamas with attached "feet" for sufficient length; if they restrain the toes, cut the seams open.
- Keep bed coverings and blankets loose around the foot area.
- Allow your child to stand and walk naturally when ready. Using prewalking aids that force your child to assume positions he or she is unable to support can harm growth centers in the foot, leg, hip, and back.

PRESCHOOL AND SCHOOL-AGE CHILDREN. Children's feet have a way of growing at irregular intervals. They may not change for almost a year and then grow two sizes in four months. The shape of a shoe should follow the actual shape of your child's foot as closely as possible. Well-designed shoes are usually long, straight, sleek, and without a lot of clutter. The most popular style of children's shoe is athletic or tennis shoes. Children can wear these in all kinds of climates except the very coldest. All athletic shoes have limited durability, and rarely do they last more than a year, but many of the cheaper brands seem to fall apart much more quickly. Check the condition of your child's tennis shoes frequently.

Popular, classically styled children's shoes include brogues, oxfords, loafers, docksiders, Mary Janes, and ballerina slippers.

When little boys begin to walk, an oxford-style shoe is usually selected. White, navy, brown and white, or black and white are the traditional colors. Although white is not always easy to keep clean, white or partly white shoes usually look better on a small child than dark colors such as brown or black. By the time boys reach school age, classically styled oxfords, loafers, and docksiders are smart choices. These all look very nice with school and dress-up clothes. Hush Puppies and similar suede shoes work well for most occasions.

Some boys' shoes have particularly thick soles, but thick soles are not necessary. In fact, children like athletic shoes because of their flexible soles. The firm soles of other shoes may become quite uncomfortable.

Dressy shoes for girls classically resemble Mary Janes or ballet slippers. Black or white patent leather for winter or summer will go with most dress-up looks. Simplicity is the rule of good taste; avoid too many buckles, bows, straps, or details.

Penny loafers, docksiders, and ducks also fit today's active young ladies, but they don't go well with dressy party clothes. A classic sandal can adapt to summer dresses, but in the winter a more sophisticated shoe is necessary, particularly for older girls.

Shoelaces were invented to drive both kids and adults crazy. For many children the art of tying shoes doesn't include the knowledge of how to *keep* shoes tied. There is no absolute answer to this problem, unfortunately, since many young children lack the manual dexterity to pull the loops tightly when they tie a shoe. Double knots usually help, but children still need to practice tying correctly, since around second grade children get embarrassed if they have knots in their shoelaces.

How can you tell if the shoe fits?

- Measure both feet.
- Have your child wear socks to be used with the new shoes.

- Fit the larger foot.
- Check fit when the child is standing and both shoes are completely laced.
- Press toe area with your thumb: there should be about 1/2″ between the end of the longest toe and the tip of the shoe.
- Test the width of the shoe by pinching the upper material around the ball of the foot and pulling it up at the vamp: you should get about 1/4″ of "extra" material in your fingers.
- Be certain the ball of the foot is at the widest part of the shoe.

Although there is no standard guide to the rate of foot growth, check the feet as follows:

FOOT GROWTH CHECKLIST

When your child is age ...	*Check fit of his or her shoes every...*
1 to 6 years	1 to 2 months
7 to 10 years	2 to 3 months
11 to 12 years	3 to 4 months
13 to 15 years	4 to 5 months
16 to 20 years	6 months

Once your child has outgrown high tops, he or she will want to wear other styles. In selecting shoes, be aware of the fit characteristics of different models. Here are some important features to look for in well-made shoes for older children:

- Neat finishing, no loose threads or rough surfaces
- Folded and stitched topline
- 1/4″ sole for play shoes; thinner sole for dress shoes
- Firm heel counter
- Scuff-resistant toe caps
- Padding under heel
- A cast buckle, attached to an elastic gore
- Fully lined straps, with at least five holes
- Welted (stitched) sole construction on play shoes

BELTS

A classically designed leather belt will last for a long time. Simple, clean lines with plainer buckles and a minimum of decorations will give children the most use. Large buckles, fancy tooled leathers, and extremely wide belts may be fad items at times, but they go out of style fast. If your child is very thin, or slim in the hips, an elastic belt may help his or her clothes fit better. Belts that are adjustable last longer, since they can yield to growth.

A belt with a contrasting color can improve and update a basic wardrobe. One little girl, Susie, loved purple but didn't have any basic clothes in that color. Her mother bought Susie a purple belt to wear with the basic tans and blues she had in her wardrobe. Susie was extremely happy with this compromise.

UNDERWEAR

Children's underwear styles follow adult trends. Be sure that your child's underwear fits properly, not only for his own comfort and hygiene, but also because his clothes will hang better. Underwear is a great clothing group to have fun with: it gives you lots of room to play with the latest fads.

UNDERPANTS. Underpants for girls come in two basic styles: the bikini and the brief. Although both styles are popular with girls, the bikini type really only looks good on very slim children without visible tummies. Most girls' underwear is made of cotton or nylon. Crotches in all underpants should be cotton because cotton absorbs moisture. Also, since cotton is a less heat-sensitive fiber, cotton panties can be washed and bleached at high temperatures. Underpants come in all colors, and in elaborate prints and patterns. Neutral shades are more practical, especially if your child is wearing pants or a skirt in a light color.

There are two styles of underwear for boys: the popular jockey shorts and the more traditional boxer shorts. Jockeys come in cotton and in a cotton-polyester blend. Getting the correct size is important; follow the sizing charts on the packages.

SLIPS. Half slips, petticoats, and full slips for older girls give a smooth shape to clothes, eliminate clinging from static electricity, and keep garments opaque. Antron III nylon fibers have an antistatic or noncling characteristic built into the yarn. This further prevents clinging and riding up. Slip sizes usually correspond to regular dress sizes.

UNDERSHIRTS. Undershirts are worn by both boys and girls, especially in cool climates. The most practical type has short sleeves and a round neck and is composed of knitted cotton or a cotton-poly blend. Some girls' undershirts have scooped necks, no sleeves, and lace trim. Undershirts are usually worn under clothing for warmth, but the fancier ones can also be worn alone as a camisole. In prepuberty, some girls wear undershirts for modesty.

BRAS. Bras, of course, always need to be tried on to see if they fit. This is especially true of adolescent girls, who can grow quite quickly. Comfort and support are the two important watchwords here. Training bras by Teenform in a variety of styles are available in most stores.

Girls who are just making the transition to bras can be quite sensitive about the subject, so handle it gently and compassionately. Sandy, the mother of ten-year-old Lisa, remembers vividly her shopping trip with her own mother to purchase her first bra. Sandy's mother had decided that her daughter was physically developing and needed to be rid of her undershirts and change to a training bra. But her mother had never discussed it with her and did not mention it until they were in the store. In the dressing room, Sandy was left clinging tearfully to her pink knit undershirt, painfully shy about being fitted for her first bra.

When it came time for Sandy to approach the subject with her own daughter, she did it in a much more sensitive manner. She took the time to explain to her daughter Lisa the reasons why women wear bras and suggested to Lisa that she might want to change from undershirts to a training bra sometime soon. Consequently, Lisa felt comfortable with her own body as she entered puberty and was not overly modest and self-conscious with her friends as she was maturing. And the trip to get her first bra went smoothly and happily.

WINTER ACCESSORIES

Kids seem to be constantly losing their mittens and hats, but winter accessories are among the most important items in your child's wardrobe. An improperly clothed child can get sick very easily in the winter; of course you want to prevent this.

Our neighbor received a note from the principal of her daughter's school saying that Jennifer was not wearing a hat and gloves outside in below-zero weather. Of course, Jennifer's mother had given her a hat and gloves, but Jennifer's classmates were in the habit of going without them on the playground. And so the little girl followed suit, suffering through the extreme cold and numbness. If the weather is cold or wet, put protection and warmth above all else. Even if your child complains that "no one else wears a hat," you should still insist that she wear it. It's true that winter clothing is often a pain; it looks bulky and seems to take forever to put on or take off (especially for kids). But you can't sacrifice health to looks or convenience.

Be careful, though, not to make the opposite mistake. Don't overdress your child in the winter. This can be constrictive and uncomfortable, and it may inhibit your child's ability to run around and have fun. And such overdressing is unnecessary. Overdressing toddlers and infants can even cause heat rash in cold-winter climates.

It is all right if your child is a little bit underdressed for the weather, if he or she feels comfortable and is in good health. Children usually do not get as chilled by the cold as adults do, so if it is 30 degrees outside and your son wants to wear his autumn jacket, you shouldn't worry about it. But if it gets much colder, insist that he wear his winter coat.

<u>*MITTENS AND GLOVES*</u>. Mittens are warmer than gloves because the fingers are able to warm each other, but gloves give more freedom of movement for older children. Give your child

(Photo: Merona Sport)

the choice of gloves or mittens as soon as she or he is big enough to fit into gloves. Mittens and gloves occasionally come with a yarn connecting them; this can be threaded through your child's coat and will help the mittens or gloves from being lost. With young children, this solution works well, and it is worth adding the yarn if the gloves or mittens do not already come with it. Mitten clips can also be used for the same purpose, but most children hate them and refuse to wear them. Once your child is in first grade, you should get rid of yarns and clips; your child will still lose her or his gloves, but the yarn or clips will undoubtedly be ridiculed by other children. Be sure to buy items that are waterproof and nonslip, as well as good and warm. 3M's Gore-Tex is now used to moisture-proof gloves and other outerwear.

HATS AND FACEMASKS. Hats will help keep your child warm more than any other accessory. In colder climates, protecting your child's ears is essential; knitted caps are the most versatile. For subzero weather, facemasks provide additional protection. The most practical fabric for both hats and facemasks is an acrylic knit, which resembles wool but is washable. Woolen hats and facemasks are warmer but more expensive, and they usually cannot be thrown into the washer.

BOOTS. In milder climates, basic hiking Frye or cowboy boots will do fine in most winter weather, although your child may still need galoshes on really wet days. In very cold climates, moon boots provide the heaviest insulation and protection for children's feet. The styles that seem to work best are the ones with the simplest designs and with as few laces, snaps and ties as possible. Look for classic styles in neutral colors. Insulated linings that can be removed and thrown in the dryer are an excellent feature for children who always seem to bring the snow inside with them. It is usually worth the money to buy a good pair of boots, because they will last longer, look better, and give better protection.

According to a recent article in *McCalls* magazine, dressing kids in layers of clothing is the secret to keeping them warm, because layers trap air warmed by the body. "Fabrics that breathe, such as wool and wool blends are best," the article states, "because they don't allow body moisture to become trapped next to the skin."

SOCKS AND TIGHTS

All children seem to go through socks at an unbelievable pace, either by wearing them out before they have outgrown them or by losing one of a pair. Athletic or tube socks work well for most casual clothing for both boys and girls. White or gray are the most popular and versatile colors. Buy socks made of cotton or cotton blends (at least 50 percent cotton, blended with other fibers). These cushion the foot well and generally absorb moisture. Dark dress socks for boys look best for special occasions. Dark heather tones of lighter-weight dress socks are also a good choice; they can be worn with a variety of dressy outfits. Argyles and small patterned socks are fashionable, but still classic.

For girls, leg wear in particular has become more than a basic accessory. Layered-leg dressing, first popular with adults, has really caught on with kids. Items currently in style include

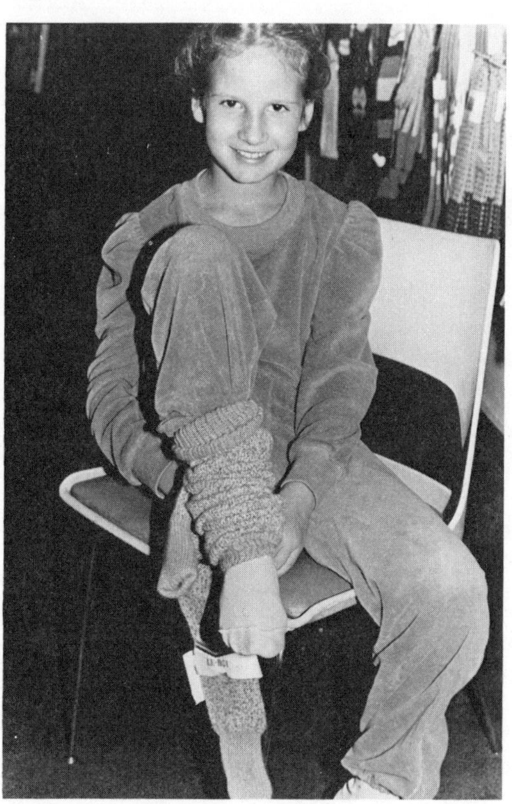

tights, socks, leg warmers, and spats, each of which can add color and dash to the most basic outfit. In tights or knee socks, classic black or white works well with most outfits. Colored leg wear in bright tones can add interest; solid colors work best for most coordinated clothing. Patterns can look awkward on children with heavier legs. Too many patterns can also be confusing for younger children who are trying to put together an outfit themselves. Cable-knit tights, however, are warmer than plain tights.

Leg warmers in assorted patterns can combine with solid tights to update even the oldest hand-me-downs. With dressy dresses, white tights or anklets consistently provide an elegant look. As white tights become worn, they can be used for playing, but it is a good idea to always keep one nice pair of white tights for those dress-up occasions.

JEWELRY

With children, a little bit of jewelry goes a long way. Keep it simple, but still allow for novelty items and trends such as rings, name bracelets, and necklaces. On younger children, jewelry will add more fun than beauty to their appearance, but we still advise staying away from the really gaudy stuff. As children reach school age, a watch becomes a basic necessity.

EYEWEAR

With anyone who is the least bit vain, glasses are a sore point. For kids, the issue looms larger, since they often begin to wear glasses at an age when they are particularly self-conscious, and they have to first get used to the idea of wearing glasses at all. With the wide selection of frames available today, however, you and your child shouldn't have trouble finding a flattering pair. Plastic frames are safer for children. (All children are active, so even if the child is not involved in sports, she or he is apt to participate in classroom shenanigans and accidentally get bumped.) For the athletic child, keep durability in mind. A plastic frame with spring-loaded hinges and scratch-resistant plastic lenses or impact-resistant lenses are ideal.

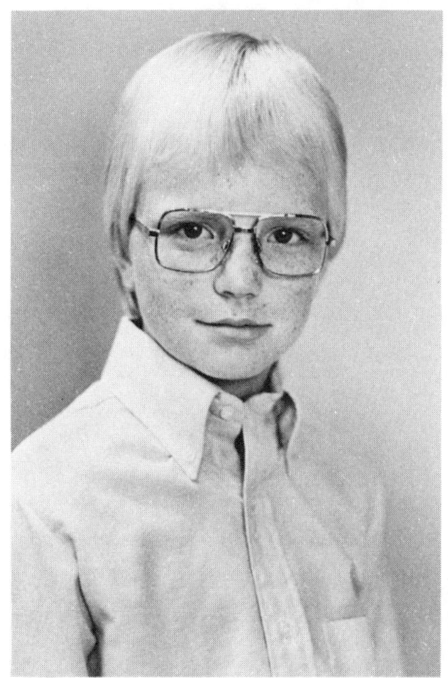
(Photo: Fifth Avenue Eyewear)

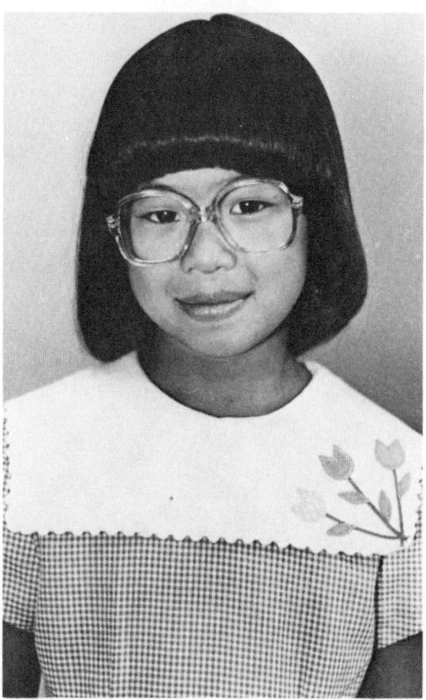
(Photo: Fifth Avenue Eyewear)

Here are some tips for purchasing glasses:

1. Make sure the glasses are not too tight around the ears or on the bridge of the nose. This tightness can cause redness and even bruises or cuts.
2. The glasses should rest firmly on top of your child's nose. They should not slip down, even when your child shakes his head vigorously. Glasses that slip don't fit properly. They should either be adjusted, or some other frames should be selected.
3. Certain styles of glasses are just as classic as button-down shirts or blazers. Try to purchase frames that will stay in style for years to come. Your optician can show you which styles have remained popular year after year.
4. Simple lines work best for children's glasses. Avoid frames with unusual twists and curves or with more than the simplest decorations.
5. Lenses of children's glasses are made of either unbreakable plastic or glass coated with a finish that makes them shatterproof. Plastic lenses, which are lighter than the glass ones, are by far the most popular choice. On kids' glasses, a scratch resistant finish is usually added to the plastic lens.

Heavy frames overwhelm this boy's face. A smaller pair with partial wire rims fit his face better and make his dark eyes more visible. (Photo: Fifth Avenue Eyewear)

The basic idea in selecting glasses is that they should fit your child's face. Because a child who needs glasses will probably wear them most or all of the time, it is a good idea to choose frames in a neutral shade. But that doesn't mean that a colored frame can't be neutral for some children.

Molly is a sensitive nine-year-old who found out that she was nearsighted when she was tested in the fourth grade. She was very worried that if she showed up to class wearing glasses, the other kids would make fun of her. She found a bright cherry red frame that was classically shaped and looked lovely on. The cheerful color was bright and flattering to her fair complexion, and every bit as neutral for her as her brother's brown tortoise-shell glasses were for him. Because the frames were special, Molly forgot her shyness and felt completely comfortable wearing her glasses all the time.

Some children dislike wearing glasses, and some eye specialists therefore suggest contact lenses for children at an early age. In many cases, contact lenses can vastly improve your child's field of vision. The big problems with contact lenses, of course, are that they are expensive and can be easily lost, especially by children. All recommendations for contact lenses should come from a vision specialist.

Part III
Fitting and Feeling Right

Measuring and Sizing Your Child

FOR YOUR CHILDREN TO LOOK their best, their clothes need to fit them well. However, you are not about to have your child's clothes tailor-made. Since you will be purchasing your son's or daughter's clothing off the racks, you should always have some idea of his or her sizes for pants, shirts and blouses, skirts, dresses, socks, shoes, and so on.

It is very important to measure your child just before you go shopping for clothes. Children grow quickly and often in short spurts, so a measurement taken even a month ago may no longer be accurate. This is particularly true of adolescents. A twelve-year-old boy may have been wearing the same pair of pants for a year, and suddenly, almost overnight, they are four inches too short for him.

Some parents don't measure their children, but simply take them to the store and have them try several different sizes on. This wastes time. For one thing, children get tired and irritable from shopping (especially clothes shopping) very quickly and easily. So do mothers and fathers. Therefore, the less time your child spends putting on and taking off clothes, the more cheerful everyone is likely to be, especially if your child is hard to fit or if it takes a while to find clothes that both you and he or she like.

Measuring your child beforehand takes only a minute or two, but a child can easily spend five minutes or more trying on and removing one button-down shirt, particularly as he or she gets older and wants privacy in the dressing room.

Children's sizes do vary from one brand of clothing to another, just as adult sizes do. Your daughter may take a size 7 pair of Gloria Vanderbilt jeans, a size 10 in a pair of Levi's. There is sometimes even considerable variation between two items of clothing that are the same make and supposedly the same size. There is a classic story in the clothing industry of the department store that sold out all its size 9 dresses in a certain design but that had several size 7s of that same design left over. The store sent back the size 7s to the manufacturer and ordered some size 9s in their place. The manufacturer simply removed the size-7 labels, sewed on size-9 labels, and sent the very same dresses back to the store.

Since children's clothes vary so much, your son or daughter should try on every piece of clothing you are thinking of buying, except for socks and underwear. Even sleepwear should be tried on in the store, if possible. Even if the sizes are only small, medium, and large, and your child is a very definite small, check the sizing first by trying it on.

The instance in which you don't have to try garments on is when you're buying for an infant. But even then it is a good idea to put the garment on your baby if you can—or at least to hold it up to her or his body to compare and check. Remember, it always takes less time to try something on in the store than to make a special trip to return or exchange an item.

The cut of a particular piece of clothing can also vary a good deal from one manufacturer to another. One brand of pants may fit your son just right in the seat but be too tight in the crotch; another may fit just right in the crotch but be too short in the legs. You need to do some experimenting to find the right cut and make of clothes for your child. Taking this time to find the manufacturer or manufacturers whose clothes best fit your child's proportions may be well worth the effort. Body proportions change much more slowly than regular sizing.

Do not ever buy your child clothing that, to the untrained eye, is visibly big on him or her. While it is true that your child will grow into the item, he or she will look awkward in it right

This illustration shows how body proportions change through stages of growth. In a young child, the ratio of head size to body size is one to four. In an adult, the head is one eighth the size of the body.

now. This seems like a commonsense rule. Still, we've seen many kids wearing outfits that must have looked gorgeous in the store but have little to do with the body of the wearer. The effect is ruined. And we imagine the kids know it.

We are well aware of the high price of clothes. But a garment that is too big is just as inappropriate and just as poor a fit as one that is three sizes too small.

TURNING MEASUREMENTS INTO SIZES

Following are several charts that will show you what sizes to look for to fit your child, based on his or her measurements. Although these figures are the same ones that manufacturers use in designing and producing kids' clothes, you should use them as general guides only. The only way you can truly tell whether an item fits or not is to have your child try it on.

We have provided sizing guides for children of all ages, from infants to teenagers. In most cases, we have provided separate tables for girls and boys. These guides will give you the sizes for children's shirts, blouses, pants, skirts, dresses, vests, coats and jackets, underwear, shoes and boots, and gloves.

Here are the points to remember when measuring and sizing your children:

1. In smaller children, the waist is at a higher level.
2. Most children's garments should allow between 1/4″ and 1″ of freedom for movement and comfort. The larger your child, the more freedom he or she needs.
3. Infant and toddler sizing allows room for diapers.
4. Clothing for infants and toddlers is often labeled by age. Nevertheless, your own child's actual height and weight are far more important than his or her age. If your one-year-old is large for her age, don't buy her clothing that is labeled "for 1-year-olds." Recommendations on labels are just that, recommended guidelines.
5. There are specialty sizes for chubby children and slim children. Charts for these measurements, weights, and sizes are also included.

INFANT SIZES

Clothes for infants have sizes that are the same for girls and boys. These sizes correspond to ages from birth to eighteen to thirty-six months old. Infants grow quickly and change sizes every two to three months, or even less.

INFANT SIZES AND PHYSICAL MEASUREMENTS

	Physical Parameters		
Size	Height	Weight	Chest
Newborn: birth to around 3 months	Maximum 24″	Maximum 14 lbs.	15″–17″
Small: up to 6 months	24½″–28″	15–20 lbs.	17½″–18″
Medium: up to 18 months	28½″–32″	21–26 lbs.	18½″–19″
Large: up to 24 months	32½″–36″	27–32 lbs.	19½″–21½″
Extra Large: up to 36 months	36½″–38″	33–36 lbs.	22″–24″

TODDLER SIZES

Clothing sizes for toddler boys and girls range from 1T to 4T and are appropriate for children between the ages of eighteen months and four years, although some children grow out of toddler sizes by age two or three. The "T" next to the size refers to "toddler." All these garments are cut fuller to allow room for diapers. Toddler clothing has an undefined waistline and naturally gives your child a rounded-looking tummy and a fuller appearance.

TODDLER SIZES AND PHYSICAL MEASUREMENTS

Size	Physical Parameters			
	Height	Weight	Chest	Waist
1T	29½"–32"	25 lbs.	19½"–20"	20"–20½"
2T	32½"–35"	26–29 lbs.	20½"–21"	20½"–21"
3T	35½"–38"	30–34 lbs.	21½"–22"	21"–21½"
4T	38½"–41"	35–38 lbs.	22½"–23"	21½"–22"

CHILDREN'S REGULAR SIZES

Children's regular sizes fit kids from three or four to seven or eight years old. The size range is from 2 to 6X. The clothes make children look taller and slimmer than do toddler or infant clothes, but these sizes still have an undefined waistline. Children's sizes run appropriately for both boys and girls.

CHILDREN'S REGULAR SIZES AND MEASUREMENTS

Size	Physical Parameters				
	Height	Weight	Chest	Waist	Hips
2	32½"–35"	27–29 lbs.	20½"–21¼"	20"–20½"	21½"–22"
3	35½"–38"	29½–35 lbs.	21½"–22"	20½"–21"	22½"–23"
4	38½"–41"	35½–39 lbs.	22½"–23"	21"–21½"	23½"–24"
5	41½"–44"	39½–45 lbs.	23½"–24"	21½"–22"	24½"–25"
6	44½"–47"	45½–50 lbs.	24½"–25"	22"–22½"	25½"–26"
6X	47½"–49"	50½–55 lbs.	25½"–26½"	22½"–23"	26½"–27"

CHILDREN'S SLIM SIZES

Children's slim sizes are appropriate for both girls and boys. They follow the same size and age range as children's regular sizing does, but you'll see the word *slim* marked on the label. The difference is in the hips and waist, which are cut narrower than corresponding garments in regular sizes.

CHILDREN'S SLIM SIZES AND MEASUREMENTS

Size	Height	Weight	Chest	Waist	Hips
		Physical Parameters			
2	32½"–35"	20–24 lbs.	19½"	19"	20"
3	35½"–38"	24½–26½ lbs.	20"	19½"	20½"
4	38½"–41"	27–29 lbs.	21"	20"	21"
5	41½"–44"	29½–35 lbs.	22"	20½"	21½"
6	44½"–47"	35½–39 lbs.	23"	21"	22"
6X	47½"–49"	39½–45 lbs.	23½"	21½"	22½"

CHILDREN'S SMALL, MEDIUM, AND LARGE SIZES

Children's small, medium, and large sizes are commonly found in sweaters, smocks, nightwear, and so forth. These sizes are appropriate for both girls and boys.

CHILDREN'S SMALL, MEDIUM, AND LARGE SIZES AND MEASUREMENTS

Size	Height	Weight
	Physical Parameters	
S—Small (fits sizes 2–3)	32"–38"	29–34 lbs.
M—Medium (fits sizes 4–5)	38½"–44"	35–44 lbs.
L—Large (fits sizes 6–6X)	44½"–49"	45–50 lbs.
XL—Extra Large (fits size 6X)	44"–49"	51–55 lbs.

GIRLS' REGULAR SIZES

Clothes made for girls from ages seven to eleven are geared toward a figure with an undefined bustline but a slightly defined waistline. Sizes range from 7 to 14 and sometimes a 16.

GIRLS' REGULAR SIZES AND MEASUREMENTS

	Physical Parameters					
Size	Height	Weight	Chest	Waist	Hips	Inseam Length
7	49″–51½″	55–60 lbs.	26″–26½″	22″–22½″	27″–28″	23½″
8	52″–53½″	60½–68 lbs.	27″–27½″	23″–23½″	28½″–29″	24½″
10	54″–55½″	68½–76 lbs.	28″–29″	24″–24½″	29″–30½″	25½″
12	56″–58″	76½–86 lbs.	29½″–30½″	25″–25½″	31″–32½″	26½″
14	58½″–60½″	86½–98 lbs.	31″–33″	26″–26½″	33″–34½″	27½″

GIRLS' SMALL, MEDIUM, LARGE SIZES

Girls' clothes with labels Small, Medium, and Large can be for a girl who ranges from about 50 pounds to 90 pounds.

GIRLS' SMALL, MEDIUM, AND LARGE SIZES AND MEASUREMENTS

	Physical Parameters	
Size	Height	Weight
S—Small (fits regular and slim sizes 7–8)	49″–53½″	50 lbs.–60 lbs.
M—Medium (fits regular and slim sizes 10–12)	54″–58″	65 lbs.–80 lbs.
L—Large (fits regular and slim size 14)	58½″–60½″	85 lbs.–90 lbs.

GIRLS' SLIM SIZES

Clothes that range from 7 slim to 14 slim for girls are characterized by a lean cut, undefined bustline, and a defined waistline similar to Girls' Regular.

GIRLS' SLIM SIZES AND MEASUREMENTS

	Physical Parameters					
Size	Height	Weight	Chest/Bust	Waist	Hips	Inseam Length
7 Slim	49"–51½"	50–53 lbs.	24"–24½"	20½"–21"	25½"–26"	23½"
8 Slim	52"–53½"	53½–59 lbs.	25"–25½"	21½"–22"	26½"–27"	24½"
10 Slim	54"–55½"	59½–67 lbs.	26"–27"	22½"–23"	27½"–28½"	25½"
12 Slim	56"–58"	67½–77 lbs.	27½"–28½"	23½"–24"	29"–30"	26½"
14 Slim	58½"–60½"	77½–89 lbs.	29"–30"	24½"–25"	31"–31½"	27½"

BOYS' SIZES

Sizes 7–12 are for boys ages five to twelve.

BOYS' SIZES AND MEASUREMENTS

	Physical Parameters				
Size	Chest	Waist	Hips/Seat	Neckband	Approximate Height
7	26"	23"	27"	11¾"	48"
8	27"	24"	28"	12"	50"
10	28"	25"	29½"	12½"	54"
12	30"	26"	31"	13"	58"

TEEN BOYS' SIZES

Teen sizes in boys' clothing are for boys age ten or twelve to adult, and are geared to the tall, maturing boy.

TEEN BOYS' SIZES AND MEASUREMENTS

Size	Chest	Waist	Hips/Seat	Neckband	Approximate Height
			Physical Parameters		
14	32″	27″	32½″	13½″	61″
16	33½″	28″	34″	14″	64″
18	35″	29″	35½″	14½″	66″
20	36½″	30″	37″	15″	68″

SOCK SIZES

The following table will be helpful when you buy socks for your child.

SOCK SIZE FOR BOYS AND GIRLS

Shoe Size	Approximate Age	Sock Size
0	3 months	4
1–2	6 months	4½
2½–3	9 months	5
3½–4½	1 year	5½
5–6	1½ years	6
6½–7½	2–3 years	6½
8–9	3–4 years	7
9½–10½	4–5 years	7½
11–12	5–6 years	8
12½ –1½	7–8 years	8½
2–3½	8–9 years	9
4–5½	9 years and above	9½

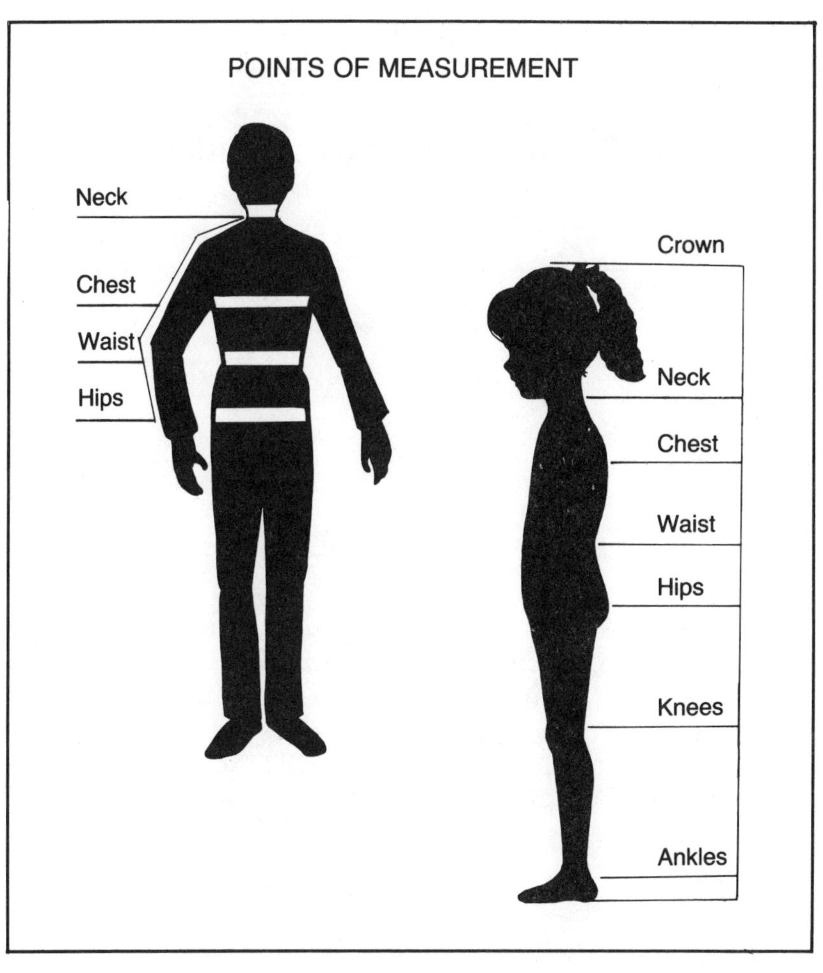

POINTS OF MEASUREMENT
Neck
Chest
Waist
Hips
Crown
Neck
Chest
Waist
Hips
Knees
Ankles

8

Fabrics and Fibers

Fabrics vary widely in durability, ease of care, comfort, cost, and beauty. To make an informed decision about the clothes you buy for your kids, you should be aware of the characteristics—positive and negative—of the materials of which they are made. This chapter gives you the basics of fabrics, fibers, and clothing finishes.

FIBERS

Fibers are the hairlike substances from which yarn and thread are made. Fibers can be either natural or synthetic (human-made). The natural fibers come from plants (for example, cotton from cotton plants, linen from flax) and animals (for example, silk produced by silkworms, wool from sheep). Synthetic fibers are chemically created. These include nylon, polyester, and acrylics.

Every article of new clothing sold in stores should have a label that lists exactly what fiber or fibers it is made of. If more than one fiber has been used, the percentage of each fiber must also be listed on the label. (Fibers making up less than 5 percent of the total garment need not be listed, however.)

In adult clothing today, the trend is a return to natural fibers.

74

Children's wear usually is made of a blend of natural and synthetic fibers or is made of 100 percent synthetic fibers, although in some high-fashion children's wear, purely natural fibers are also being used.

The fiber or fibers used in an item of clothing determine how it holds its shape, how durable it is, what kind of washing, drying, and ironing is appropriate, and how stains and spots can be removed from it. Clothing care, maintenance, and stain removal will be discussed in detail in Chapter 14.

All fibers possess certain basic characteristics, and knowing these characteristics will really help you to determine which fabrics are best for a particular garment. For example, if you are looking for an undershirt for your child, you will want a soft, absorbent fiber, such as cotton, rather than something nonabsorbent, such as nylon. However, in a winter ski jacket, the best choice of fabrics would be nylon, which has greater strength and wear-resistance than cotton.

Synthetic fibers blended with natural fibers will contain the good points of each type of fiber. It is important to know the percentage of each fiber because that determines which characteristics will predominate. For example, a shirt or blouse made of an 80/20 cotton/polyester blend will be fairly comfortable, durable and able to breathe pretty well. A 100 percent polyester blouse will be still more durable, but unable to let much air pass through. A 100 percent cotton blouse will not be as durable as either of the other two blouses, but it will breathe extremely well and absorb moisture better than the other two.

NATURAL FIBERS. The most commonly used natural fibers are cotton, linen, wool, and silk.

Cotton is the single most common fiber in children's clothing. It is fairly inexpensive, extremely versatile, and comfortable. Cotton wrinkles easily because of its elasticity. Therefore, many children's garments are made of a blend of cotton and a synthetic fiber such as polyester, which is less likely to wrinkle. Sometimes a wrinkle-resistant finish is added to cotton. Cotton can mildew and shrink.

Linen comes from the stem of the flax plant and is generally considered the oldest textile fiber. It has excellent strength and absorbency. Linen is a lint-free fabric because the fibers themselves are very long. Like cotton, linen can mildew, and it may shrink when it is washed. Linen is not found frequently in children's clothing because it is quite expensive and requires more care.

Wool has good elasticity and resilience. It is a warm fabric because the fibers interlock in a mass when they are washed or when they are exposed to heat and moisture. Because wool is an expensive fiber, it is normally used only in better children's clothing. Wool clothing wears well, and wool clothes are usually quality clothes.

There are two types of wool fibers: *woolen* and *worsted.* Woolen yarns are short, curly, and bulky. They are soft, thick, and fuzzy in appearance. Most children's wool sweaters are made from woolen yarn.

Worsted wools wrinkle less and are more durable than woolens. Worsted fibers are long, straight, and firm, and they have a hard finish. A child's blazer would probably be made of worsted yarns.

The two labels shown below (right) are symbols of quality, which are found on fine wool clothes. They indicate the amount of wool in the fabric and that the garment meets the specifications of the Wool Bureau.

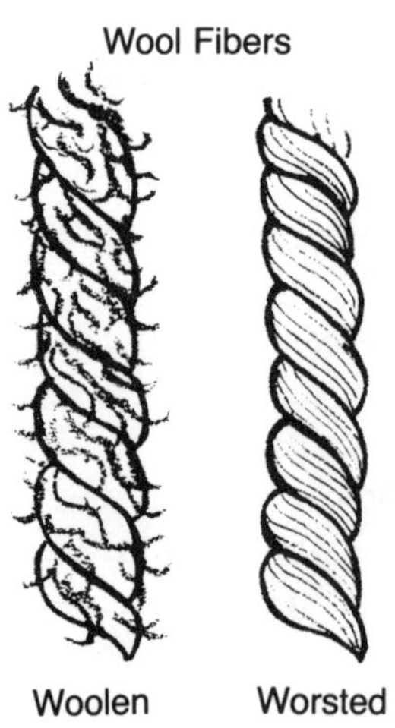

Silk comes from the cocoons of the silkworms. Cultivated mainly in eastern Asia, it is elegant, costly, and beautiful. Of all the natural fibers, silk is the strongest. It drapes well and has a luxurious feel; however, it has only fair resiliency and may wrinkle. It is used for scarves, blouses, dresses, and jackets, but its cost is often prohibitive in children's clothing.

SYNTHETIC FIBERS. Synthetic fibers have been in existence since the late nineteenth century, but only recently have they become a major commercial product. The first human-made fiber produced in the United States was rayon, which appeared in 1910. Rayon is produced from cellulose plant fibers, which are processed to resemble many different natural fibers.

Since the 1940s, a large number of new synthetic fibers have been developed. Their many different brand names can often be confusing for consumers. However, generic family names have been given to these fibers, and these have helped considerably in identifying the many brand names and the characteristics of each. A table of fibers and their characteristics follows.

YARNS

When fibers are twisted together in a continuous strand, they are called *yarns*. These yarns are then woven or knitted to make fabrics, from which all clothing is made. People often refer to yarns as thread, but yarn is the proper term.

Yarns can be combined, looped, or processed to produce a variety of textures. For example, better cotton yarns like *percale* will go through an additional combing process after the fibers have been carded. Carding is a basic process that straightens and smooths fibers before they are twisted into yarns. Combing, then, is a second step that gets rid of short fibers, leaving only the longer, smoother ones. The result is a fabric that feels smoother and drapes better. *Muslin* is another cotton yarn, but it is much rougher in texture. It may wrinkle more easily than percale, and it even has slight specks and surface irregularities. It is made of carded yarns, not combed yarns like percale.

Yarns are also classified as single or ply yarns. A ply yarn is made up of two or more single yarns twisted together. Ply yarns help a garment hold its shape; they also reduce *pilling*, which

SUMMARY OF TEXTILE FIBERS

Fiber	Chief Uses	Characteristics	Precautions
NATURAL FIBERS			
Cotton	Light- and medium-weight apparel Household textiles	Versatile Durable Can withstand frequent hard laundering Is easily ironed at high temperature	Protect stored items against dampness to prevent mildew
Linen	Women's and children's blouses and dresses; summer suiting Handkerchiefs Table linens Other household fabrics	Beauty and luster endure through frequent hard launderings Does not shed lint May be more expensive than cotton Wrinkles easily unless treated to resist wrinkling Resistant to dye-type stains	For best wear, do not press in sharp creases Protect stored items against dampness to prevent mildew For smooth appearance, iron at high temperature
Silk	Light- and medium-weight apparel Accessory items such as scarves Some expensive upholstery and drapery fabrics	Has natural luster and strength Is moderately resilient to wrinkles and readily returns to shape Dyes well Is more expensive than synthetic (filament) silky yarns Some items may be carefully hand-laundered	To clean most items, dry-clean Protect from prolonged exposure to light Protect against moths and carpet beetles
Wool	Outerwear Light, medium, or heavy-weight apparel	Springs back into shape; requires little pressing Has great versatility in fabrics and colors Has insulating capacity that increases with fabric thickness; hence fabric can be warm or cold	Dry-clean most items Never wash woolens in hot water. Moist heat and agitation as in some laundering will shrink and felt wool Protect against moths and carpet beetles

Fiber	Chief Uses	Characteristics	Precautions
SYNTHETIC FIBERS			
Acetate	Light- and medium-weight apparel Fiberfill	Drapes well Dries quickly Is inexpensive Is subject to fume-fading Has poor abrasion resistance Loses some strength when wet	Iron or press only at very low temperature to prevent melting and fusing of fibers
Acrylic* *Acrilan* *Creslan* *Orlon* *Zefran* *Zefkrome*	Tailored outerwear Knitted wear Pile fabrics	Resists wrinkling and effects of sunlight Has high bulking power and soft	Remove oily stains before washing; waterborne stains will come out easily Some fabrics have silky texture
Modacrylic* *Dynel* *Verel* *Elura* *SEF*	Deep pile and fleece fabrics	Resists wrinkling Resists chemicals Is soft and resilient and noncombustible	Iron at extremely low temperatures only
Novoloid *Kynol*	Fireproof clothing and fabrics	Outstanding flame resistance Nonmelting	Precautions, if any, are not currently established
Nylon*	Hosiery, lingerie Sweaters, wind jackets, dresses	Has exceptional strength and excellent elasticity Retains permanent shape Woven fabrics are often hot and uncomfortable to wear Washes easily but tends to attract dirt High abrasion resistance	Remove oily stains before washing To maintain whiteness, use nylon whiteners on the market Press at low temperature

*In addition to specific characteristics mentioned for each fiber, those fibers marked with an * have these general properties in common: (1) moderate to high strength and resilience; (2) resistance to moths and mildew; (3) sensitivity to heat of pressing iron; (4) dimensional stability; (5) resistance to shrinking or stretching; (6) tendency to accumulate static electricity in cold, dry weather; (7) nonabsorbency; (8) good washing and drying qualities; (9) resistance to non-oily stains but retention of body oils that penetrate the fiber and are hard to remove; and (10) pleat retention because of thermoplastic qualities.

Fiber	Chief Uses	Characteristics	Precautions
Polyester* *Dacron* *Fortrel* *Kodel* *Vycron* *Anavor* *Avlin* *Blue C* *Encron* *Quintess* *Textura* *Trevira*	Wash-and-wear apparel, often in combination with other fibers Fiberfill	Has exceptional wrinkle resistance; therefore needs little ironing or pressing Easy to wash Has sharp pleat and crease retention Some fabrics resist pilling	Remove oily stains before washing Follow directions given on hang tags or care labels to keep white fabrics white
Rayon (conventional)	Light- and medium-weight clothing	Absorbent Inexpensive Moderately durable Lacks resilience; wrinkles easily Brushed or napped fabrics may be combustible	Launder carefully to prevent shrinkage or stretching; rayon does not withstand treatment that can be given cotton or linen When in doubt about the washability of garments, dry-clean
Rayon (high wet modules) *Avril* *Nupron* *Xena* *Zantrel*	Sweaters, wind jackets Dresses	Can be mercerized Has higher dry and wet strength than conventional rayon Can be washed	
Rubber *Lastex*	Foundation garments Swimwear	High degree of stretch and recovery Damaged by oils and light	Wash frequently with mild soap and detergent Avoid constant overstretching
Spandex *Glospan* *Lycra* *Numa*	Foundation garments Swimwear Ski pants, other sportswear	Has a high degree of stretch and recovery Resists abrasion Is resistant to body oils	To machine-launder, use warm water and dry on lowest heat with shortest cycle
Vinyon*	Mixed with other fibers for heat bonding	Resistant to chemicals and sunlight Noncombustible	

is the formation of tiny balls on the surface of the fabric. Pilling occurs naturally when the garment rubs against anything rough.

Yarns that have the ability to stretch are becoming increasingly popular today. Stretch fabrics, which give with each body movement, are used in jeans and active wear, as well as in swimwear, belts, leotards, and tights.

Texturizing adds to a yarn's elasticity and increases its bulk.

FABRIC PRODUCTION

Most fabrics are made by either *weaving* or a *knitting* process.

WOVEN FABRICS. Woven fabrics are produced by two sets of yarns interlaced at right angles on a loom. There are three basic types of fabric weaving: *plain*, *twill*, and *satin* weaving.

A plain weave interlaces yarns in a checkerboard fashion. This type of weave is relatively inexpensive and is quick and easy to produce. If the weave is tight, a strong fabric results. Most children's clothing is made of common, plain-weave fabrics such as *gingham*, *percale*, *chintz*, *homespun*, *taffeta*, or *organdy*.

A twill weave differs from a plain weave in its appearance as well as in its construction. A twill weave is formed by passing a yarn backward as well as forward. If you examine a twill woven fabric closely, you'll notice that the weave creates a staircase pattern. This construction method produces closer, tighter, stronger fabrics. Some examples of twill weave fabrics used in children's wear include *denim*, *gabardine*, *chino*, *tweed*, *flannel*, and *whipcord*.

The satin weave is not to be confused with the lustrous fabric of the same name. The satin weaving process produces a fabric with a high sheen and a smooth surface that looks like satin. Although this creates an attractive appearance, a satin weave has several disadvantages: weaker fabric construction, less durability, and the possibility of snagging. Because of these disadvantages, satin weave fabrics are not very useful for most children's garments.

Which weave makes the strongest fabric? The more yarns per inch a fabric has, the stronger it will be. Generally speaking, twill weaves are stronger than plain weaves, and they are both more durable than satin weaves. But you should examine the fabric closely on any item you are thinking of purchasing. A tight plain weave may be a better, stronger fabric than a loose, poorly constructed twill.

To check the quality of a fabric, simply turn a portion of a garment inside out. Look at how many interlacing yarns there are, and note how tight the weave is. You will be able to recognize both these characteristics immediately simply by looking closely. If you are uncertain how tight a weave is in comparison with other fabrics or garments, look at the inside of a few other items of clothing.

When checking for the quality of a weave, also check to make sure there are not too many loose threads. Hanging threads are the sign of a poorly made garment, and you should probably pass it by. (See Chapter 9 for a complete discussion on checking the quality of a garment.)

KNIT FABRICS. Knitting is the second most common method of fabric production. Knit fabrics are created by looping and interlooping one or more yarns. Knitted loops are called *stitches*. Vertical columns of stitches are called *wales*; horizontal rows are referred to as *courses*.

There are two main kinds of knitted fabrics. Each is knitted on a particular kind of machinery. In *weft knitting*, the yarns run horizontally across the width of the fabric. Popular weft-knitted fabrics include *jersey* (also called single knit), *rib knit*, and *purl knit*. In *warp knitting* the yarns form a vertical-look pattern and interlock diagonally.

Knit fabrics are hugely popular today because they are versatile and comfortable and because they stretch. Knits provide ease of movement, warmth, and easy fit. Many garments for infants and young children are made of knitted fabrics. Europeans use fine knits for children of all ages.

FINISHES. Finishes are the processes and treatments that a fabric undergoes after it has been woven or knitted together. These final touches can make a fabric more suitable for its intended use. Finishing can make a fabric wrinkle-resistant, water-resistant, stain-resistant, softer, crisper, shrink-proof, or otherwise more durable or attractive.

Here is a list of the most commonly used finishes:

Antistatic. These finishes help keep clothes from clinging. Chemical substances that reduce static electricity by absorbing small amounts of moisture are applied at the mill.

Antiseptic. Chemical agents are added to inhibit bacterial growth in the garment. These finishes hold up under both dry-cleaning and laundering, but they sometimes have an odor, and they can cause skin irritation.

Crease-resistant. This process is used mainly on cotton, rayon, and linen. Resins are baked into the fabric to make it more resistant to wrinkling. This process also makes fabrics stiffer and less absorbent; this can be a plus or a minus.

Embossing. A special embossing effect is easily produced by passing fabric between heated rollers. These rollers imprint designs on fabric in a sort of "waffle iron" effect. The designs used for embossing resemble more costly woven patterns, but they stay in the fabric only temporarily.

Flame-resistant and flame-retardant. These finishes are used very often on children's sleepwear, and they are an important safety feature in such clothing. Flame-retardant finishes can be built right into some synthetic fibers; these last indefinitely. Flame-retardant finishes are also available for cotton clothing; these will last through about fifty washings.

Glazing. A shiny, highly glazed fabric surface can be created by using starches, sizing, or resins, along with a simple heated-roller process. The results are fairly long lasting but not permanent.

Napping. This finish is created when the fabric is passed against rotating wire brushes. Napping results in additional insulation and softness.

Permanent press (durable press). These finishes enable a garment to resist wrinkles during both wearing and washing. Permanent creases or pleats can also be heat-set into fabrics. Some permanent press garments have a slight fishy odor, caused by the resin used in the permanent press process.

Soil-release finishes. These finishes make fibers more water-absorbent and more resistant to stains, including oil stains. Stains and soil can be removed more easily from garments that have this kind of finish.

Shrinkage-controlled. Several effective shrinkage-control finishes can help a garment retain its original size and shape. Preshrinking also controls additional shrinkage. However, even after fabrics have been preshrunk or treated, some additional shrinkage may occur. Sanforizing is the most common shrink-resistant finish used today.

Water-repellant and waterproofed. Water-repellant finishes permit the passage of air from the body, yet inhibit the penetration of water through the fabric. Water-repellant finishes can be added to a garment by most dry cleaners. Such a finish is not permanent but is, nevertheless, a valuable addition to many outerwear garments. Fabrics can also be completely waterproofed to provide the best possible protection from all types of weather. However, waterproofed garments tend to become uncomfortable if you wear them for long, because no air can get through the waterproofing. The new Gore-Tex laminates waterproof fabrics completely but also let them breathe. Gore-Tex is being used more and more in outerwear, camping equipment, and even in hiking shoes and boots.

SHRINKAGE

Different fabrics will shrink differently when washed. Some fabrics do not shrink at all. You should of course take shrinkage into account when buying your child's clothes.

Fabric blends will shrink in relation to the yarns that make them up. A 50/50 cotton/rayon blend will shrink less than cotton but more than rayon—about halfway in between the two. An 80/20 polyester/cotton blend will shrink just a little bit more than pure polyester.

9

Quality in Children's Clothing

WHILE TASTE IS A MATTER OF opinion, quality can be verified. However, it takes a trained eye to see and search for sound construction, simplicity in design, and the finest in fabrication.

Not only in children's wear, but in every merchandise category, the first consideration in the minds of both consumers and manufacturers is shifting from price to quality. "Planned simplicity"—the decision to buy and fully enjoy a few very high-quality goods, instead of a greater number of cheaper things—is the approach that more and more people are taking. Manufacturers are responding, and this means that lots of high-quality kids' clothes will be available to parents in the next few years.

Many different makes of children's clothing are available. Some of these makes are excellent; others are sheer junk; quite a few are somewhere in between. This chapter will help teach you to recognize quality in children's clothing and accessories when you see it. It will also teach you how to spot and weed through the junk, and how to avoid the artificially overpriced garment in order to find one with honest style and value.

Quality usually costs more. A well-designed and well-made shirt might be more expensive than a shoddily made one in the same general style. But although an item might have a higher price tag, it is often cheaper in the long run because of its attractiveness and durability. In fact, usually your best clothing buys are high-quality items.

The true value of a piece of clothing is determined by both the price and by how much actual use your child gets out of it. Therefore, the fabric, the weave, durability, and overall quality all play important parts in determining the real value of a garment.

Checking the quality of a garment is not difficult to do, and it is a must if you want to avoid lots of trips back to the store to return items. First, examine the outside of the garment. Check to see that the plaids, stripes, and patterns match across all seams and pockets. Check for flaws such as missed stitches, loose threads, and decorations or trim that is not firmly attached. This last test should be done by feel, not just by sight. Hunt for possible tears or holes, especially in high-stress areas, such as the seam that joins the sleeve to the body of a shirt or blouse. Look for spots, stains, and flaws in the fabric.

Next, turn the garment inside out and check the neatness of the construction. Never be afraid to do this, even if a salesperson is watching. It is entirely your right as a shopper, and it's a time-tested way to check quality. In general, the more stitches per inch, the higher the quality. Hold the garment up to the light to inspect the weave. A good garment is generally made of tightly woven fabric. Inside seams should be finished to prevent unraveling.

Better garments have double stitching for reinforcement in areas of stress such as the seat, crotch, and armholes. The bottoms of the armholes should be even and should lie flat.

Look under the collar and under the edges of pockets for consistent workmanship. Quality clothing will have generous seams and hems that allow for growing room and alterations.

Next, check the finishing details. These are key clues to quality. Zippers should lie flat and straight and close tightly and easily so that they will *stay* closed on your child. (There is nothing more frustrating to a child than a zipper that won't stay closed.) The buttons and buttonholes should be well matched; they should fit tightly but button easily. Study the buttonholes carefully: poor workmanship usually shows up here. They should be well-reinforced but smooth. It drives kids crazy if their cuffs come unbuttoned all the time or if they can't button the cuffs themselves. Quality buttons are a mark of better clothing. A fine dress, coat, or sweater will come with extra buttons.

If a fabric is heavy (as in coats or jackets, for example), each button should have a stem. If snaps are used instead of buttons, be sure the snaps are easy to work and that they stay closed.

While your child is trying on an item, be sure that he or she opens and closes every snap, button, and zipper to make sure they all work well, and to make sure that he or she can handle them without help. Watch to make sure your son or daughter closes *and* opens each of these.

In children's play clothes, double rows of stitching that show on the outside are highly desirable. Reinforcement in the knees of play pants can help to extend the life of jeans or corduroys, since young children spend a great deal of time on their knees and on the floor.

Pullover jerseys, sweaters, T-shirts, and so forth, should have head openings large enough for your child's head to fit through without a great deal of pulling and tugging. This is very important for young children who are just learning to dress themselves. Your child's head should fit easily into the neck opening of any garment, including dresses and undershirts. Watch your

Double-stitched seams make play clothes more durable.

Well-designed children's clothing—such as this skirt and jacket outfit from Norma Kamali—has an ample number of pockets. (Photo: Norma Kamali)

child put the garment on and take it off. Sometimes an item of apparel may go on easily but be difficult to remove or vice versa.

Elastic cuffs on ankles or wrists should not be constricting and should fit comfortably. Elastic that is too tight or too loose anywhere becomes a constant nuisance to kids. There should not be any broken stitching around the elastic.

Pockets are very important to children of all ages and both sexes. Check to see that the pockets are stitched firmly and that they allow for easy access. Your child's hands should be able to fit into them, with room left over for rocks, frogs, candy, and other assorted treasures. Pockets should be deep enough so that things put into them will not fall back out.

Are there enough pockets in the garment? If an item of clothing, especially pants and overalls, does not have enough pockets, don't buy it!

Belts and buckles should be well put together. The belt should fit evenly, and the fabric of the belt should hold together well. Be sure there are enough properly spaced holes if the belt is not adjustable.

Pants should have enough belt loops, and they should be evenly placed. Hems of dresses and skirts need to be even from front to back. Leg openings must be big enough for your child to fit his or her feet through easily in both directions.

Signs of poor quality include decorative items (such as ribbons or flowers) that are loose or flimsily attached or decorations and trim that are nonfunctional. Linings or hems that do not lie with the garment look cheap. Loose threads and buttons that are about to fall off or that are not firmly attached are signs of low-quality clothing. Avoid clothes with plastic fasteners; they can fall apart easily in the washer or dryer.

Remember, it is possible for a high-priced item in an expensive kids' boutique to be badly made, just as it is quite possible to find a well-made and very reasonably priced item in a discount store. The same manufacturer that normally makes quality clothes can sometimes turn out a lemon. Therefore, it is essential that you inspect the quality of every article of clothing you are thinking of buying for your child.

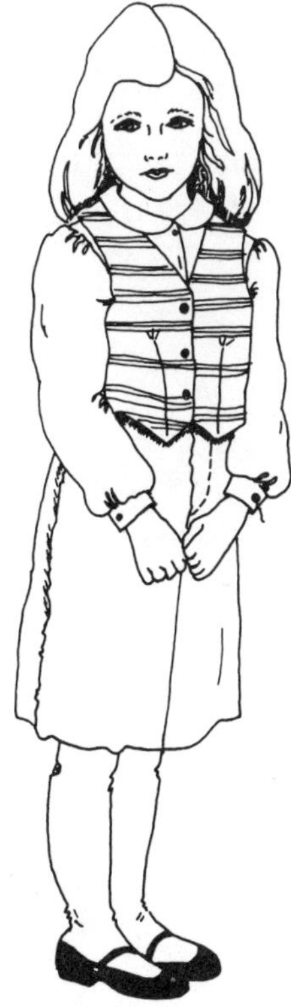

Poor Quality Giveaways

1. Shoulders too narrow

2. Missing button

3. Underarm seam too short

4. Dart puckers

5. Stripes don't match

6. Zipper puckers

7. Uneven gathers

8. Hanging threads

9. Seams pucker

10. Uneven hem

11. Socks sag

Here is a useful quality checklist. Bring it with you when you go shopping. Soon you will be able to make a sophisticated inspection without using the checklist.

<u>Checklist for Quality</u>

1. Inspect outside of garment for
   - ☐ matched seams
   - ☐ flaws
   - ☐ fabric damage
2. Inspect inside of garment for
   - ☐ neatness
   - ☐ evenness of stitches
   - ☐ finished hems
   - ☐ finished stitches
   - ☐ double stitching in stress areas
3. Zippers should
   - ☐ lie flat
   - ☐ be straight
   - ☐ close tightly
   - ☐ be easy to use
4. Buttons and buttonholes should
   - ☐ fit easily
   - ☐ be secure

Part IV
Shopping Wisely

10

What Do Kids Really Need?

CLOTHING PURCHASES ARE A major part of every family's budget. According to the U.S. Department of Agriculture, the cost to clothe a child from birth to adulthood (eighteen years old) is over $6,000.00. (See the chart on the following page.) In general, the average family of four spends about 8 percent to 10 percent of its annual income on clothing.

For most families, the clothing budget is more flexible than the budgets for food, shelter, insurance, transportation, and so on, because appropriate clothing is less of an immediate need. You must make your rent, car, and insurance payments on time, and you must eat every day, but you can do without new slacks for another few weeks, or even months.

This very flexibility, however, often leads families to overspend. You know exactly how much your mortgage payment is going to be, and you can judge from last winter what this winter's heating bill will amount to, but how much is the "right" amount to spend on your child's clothing?

We all know how easy it is to go on a spree, either for ourselves or for our children. How can anyone resist buying Kimmel that absolutely darling dress, especially when she likes it so much and it's on sale? But although that particular bargain (and others like it) may be hard to resist, there are times when you should resist them. Without careful wardrobe planning, even a bargain can be a bad investment.

ANNUAL COST OF RAISING A CHILD FROM BIRTH TO AGE EIGHTEEN (Moderate Cost Level)

Age of Child (Years)	Total*	Food	Clothing	Housing	Medical Care	Education	Transportation	Other
Under 1	$ 4,257	$ 595	$ 138	$ 1,850	$ 286	$ —	$ 824	$ 564
1	4,394	732	138	1,850	286	—	824	564
2–3	4,162	713	227	1,654	286	—	731	551
4–5	4,397	948	227	1,654	286	—	731	551
6	4,516	955	315	1,600	286	—	738	622
7–9	4,829	1,123	315	1,600	286	145	738	622
10–11	4,997	1,291	315	1,600	286	145	738	622
12	5,347	1,347	457	1,654	286	145	804	654
13–15	5,441	1,441	457	1,654	286	145	804	654
16–17	5,963	1,656	591	1,708	286	145	877	700
Total	48,303	10,801	3,180	16,824	2,860	725	7,809	6,104

*Statistics are from the U.S. Department of Agriculture, 1981

It is possible to buy high-quality clothes that look great, that your child loves to wear, and that you were able to get at bargain prices—and still spend your money unwisely. This can happen when parents buy clothes for their kids without considering carefully how those clothes will fit into and fill out their children's wardrobes. Another Shetland sweater when your daughter has three probably isn't the best choice. It's great to buy a fun and funky Kamali skirt, but if your daughter's style is down to earth and the new skirt forces you to purchase fun and funky shoes and a fun and funky top, you've lost on the exchange.

Of course, there is nothing wrong with trying to anticipate your child's needs—for instance, buying slacks on sale because you know that he or she will be needing some new slacks in a month or two. But because children sometimes can grow in great big spurts, there is always the danger that the clothes you bought two months ago may no longer fit. So be careful!

IMPULSE BUYING

Impulse buying is the trap that will surely cause you to overspend. Remember, it doesn't matter that a gorgeous blazer is on sale at $28 if your child has all the blazers he needs. Every time he wears that blazer, he is getting that much less use out of another blazer or sport jacket in his wardrobe. You are therefore spending $28 and getting little or nothing. That same $28 could instead be used to purchase something that your child genuinely *does* need. The whole point of clothing sales is to entice shoppers into buying. But do not be taken in by bargains unless the sale item is something you know your child needs and likes.

Children of all ages love fad items, and it's an unusual kid who goes through the year untouched by the various crazes that sweep the country. Parents quickly lose any susceptibility to kids' fads, once they've seen just how fast kids can lose interest in a trendy piece of clothing once the fad has run its course. From then on, lots of moms and dads are at the ready with their stock answer to excited requests for the latest fad stuff: "No we're not buying you that (<u>fill in the blank</u>). Remember the (<u>fill in the blank</u>) we bought last year? You wore it exactly three times. It's been hanging in your closet ever since. We're not pouring more money down the drain to buy things you'll hardly even use."

There's a better way to handle fads than always taking the hard line. We recommend that you indulge kids' desires to participate in current trends (they're fun, after all), but be smart when you do it. Of course, when making large purchases, avoid the fad. You don't want to buy a good sweater emblazoned with the name of the latest teenage screen idol. Fortunately, the most popular and plentiful fad items are small: T-shirts, sweat shirts, socks, barrettes, plastic wallets, costume jewelry, and hats. Take advantage of these. Your son and daughter will be delighted, you won't have overspent on junk, and when the fad is over, you'll be able to discard the item with perfect ease of mind.

HOW TO PLAN YOUR CHILD'S WARDROBE

In general, most American parents buy more clothes for their children than they need. It's better to invest in fewer, higher quality items than to have a larger number of cheap items. A well-made vest that looks good on your child will continue to look good, even if he or she wears it twice a week. A variety of different cheap outfits will look varied but cheap.

By planning your child's wardrobe in advance, you can make the most of your clothing dollar. Each child's wardrobe should be built around a core of well-made garments that work for a variety of situations and occasions and allow you to create a large number of outfits out of a relatively small number of individual pieces. Your child's three main activities during his or her waking hours are school (or day care), play, and formal occasions (church, going out to dinner, weddings and family social events, etc.). The easiest way to determine your child's clothing needs is to figure out how much time he or she spends, on the average, at each of these activities.

Not only should your child's clothes be geared to his or her activities, but they should be geared to *the amount of time spent in each activity*. For example, suppose in a typical week Michael spends about half of his time in school and school-related activities, two hours in Sunday school and church, and most of the rest of his time playing. Roughly half of Michael's clothing should then be appropriate for school, almost half should be

The activities that take up your child's time determine the kinds of outfits you'll want in his wardrobe. Here, a navy blazer and khaki pants are perfect for dressy occasions.

appropriate for play, and only a few items should be designed for church and other formal events.

Many parents build unbalanced wardrobes for their children by ignoring this principle. Michael's parents were no exception. Michael is a very handsome and distinguished-looking child; because he looks so good in coats and ties, his parents have bought him three suits, four sport jackets, and half a dozen ties.

But what makes these purchases unwise is that, although Michael looks great in formal outfits, the only places he ever wears them, with the exception of a rare wedding or other formal affair, are to church and Sunday school. So, while Michael is the best-dressed child in the congregation, he gets very little use out of each suit or coat. Michael's parents spent 35 percent of their budget for his clothes on formal wear, which Michael wears less than 5 percent of the time. Michael will grow out of all his suits and sport jackets without having gotten much use out of any of them.

Wiser purchases for Michael would have been more school clothes, more play clothes, and perhaps two or three sport jackets that could be worn on formal occasions with any of several different pairs of Michael's best school slacks. Additional variety could be created with good wool sweaters instead of sport coats.

These purchases would better reflect the actual amount of time Michael spends at each of his regular activities.

You can put this principle to work by making a list of your own child's major activities. These can be divided into three basic categories: school, play, and formal occasions. Consider how much time your child spends at each of these during a typical day, then fill out the checklist below:

_______________ 's Checklist of Daily Activities

---

1. School (includes school-related activities,   _______ hours
    such as club meetings)
2. Play   _______ hours
3. Formal occasions (church, weddings, etc.)   _______ hours

Do not include time spent in situations that require uniforms or other standardized clothing, such as parochial school, team sports, and so on. The clothing needs of your child have already been determined for these activities. Do figure in weekend activities. The point of the checklist is simply to show you what percentage of his or her waking hours your child spends in each general kind of activity.

Let's look at Jeffrey, a twelve-year-old boy, and see what his typical day looks like:

Jeffrey's Checklist of Daily Activities

School (includes school-related activities, such as club meetings)	8½ hours
Play	4 hours
Formal occasions (church, weddings, etc.)	1 hour (weekly average)

Jeffrey goes to school from 9:00 to 3:30 every day. He is involved in several different school clubs, so he spends an average of an extra hour at school each day. School is a half-hour walk away, so on a typical weekday he spends a total of about 8½ hours wearing school clothing. Jeffrey's father is a diplomat, so Jeffrey often has to dress up for formal dinners and other formal affairs. He also goes to church on Sunday mornings.

Jeffrey delivers papers for about an hour every morning, and he spends most of the rest of his time playing.

Jeffrey's parents can look at the checklist above and tell at a glance exactly how they should be spending their money on his clothing. Roughly half of the clothes they buy for Jeffrey should be suitable for school. About a third of his clothes should be play clothes. A little less than 10 percent should be suitable for formal occasions.

By filling in the amounts of time your child spends at these activities, you too can tell at a glance how much of your child's wardrobe should be devoted to each activity.

Earlier in this book we stressed the importance of buying clothes that will work in a variety of situations. If Jeffrey's parents were to buy him rugged but stylish Izod corduroy slacks and a matching sport jacket, then those slacks would function for school and for some formal occasions. They might also function as play clothes in many situations. Durable V-neck sweaters would serve him well both for school and play. Plus, if Jeffrey were to wear a button-down sport shirt and a tie along with one of the sweaters, this outfit would be appropriate for formal occasions. Thus, by thinking out Jeffrey's wardrobe in advance and making their purchases wisely, Jeffrey's parents will be able to get items that fit virtually all of Jeffrey's activities. This general principle can extend to nearly every article of Jeffrey's clothing.

Once you have filled out the checklist for your child's daily activities, look at his or her wardrobe. How closely does it fit the checklist? If the wardrobe is too limited in a certain area, that is an area in which you should concentrate your purchases next time you go shopping for your child's clothes.

When summer approaches, your child's activities will probably change a good deal, so you may need to make up a new checklist. However, if you have been purchasing versatile garments that can be worn in three of four seasons and in different situations, your child will probably need only a few additions to his or her wardrobe, despite the changes in daily activities.

HOW TO DO A WARDROBE INVENTORY

Before you go shopping for any new clothes for your child, you need to know first what she or he has, what fits and what doesn't, and what she or he needs. Until you know the answers to these questions, you don't know what you are shopping for. A wardrobe inventory will show you exactly what clothes are worn out or too damaged to be repaired, which need mending, which fit well, which fit adequately, which no longer fit at all, and which new purchases are necessary.

You should do a wardrobe inventory for each of your children twice a year. The best times are in early spring and early fall, so that you have plenty of time to plan and budget for major purchases.

Here are the steps to follow in performing a wardrobe inventory:

1. Remove all garments from your child's closet that do not fit, that she or he has not worn in the last year, or that are worn out.
2. Separate the summer and winter clothing. Put them either in separate closets or at different ends of the same closet.
3. Go carefully through each item of your child's clothes, and fill out the Inventory Form on the following page.
4. Take informal inventory of accessory items: scarves, ties, belts, hats, socks, underwear, sleepwear, handkerchiefs, robes, gloves, shoes and boots, slippers, and so forth.

Now you know exactly what your child has and what she or he needs. The next few steps can help you determine what styles, designs, and colors to look for when you shop.

5. Using the methods described in Chapter 5, decide what color or colors look best on your child. With your child's help and agreement, choose a basic color and a second color for her or him. Note which items in the current wardrobe will go well with these colors. (If your child already has a basic and a second color and does not wish to change them, you can skip this step.)
6. What clothes has your child worn that have brought her or him the most compliments? Take note of the items, styles, designs, fabrics, colors, and brand names that have generated these compliments.
7. What are the colors, styles, designs, and fads that your child likes best or most wants to wear? The one way to find out is to ask her or him.

Inventory Form

Item	Color	Description	Fit*	Condition**	Needs
Coats and jackets					
Pants					
Skirts and dresses					
Shirts and blouses					
Sweaters					

* For fit, use codes:
P—Perfect
S—Slightly small
B—Slightly big

** For condition, use codes:
W—Wearable
R—Repairable
D—Discard

11

Getting the Most for Your Clothing Dollar

ONE MAJOR TREND IN FASHION today is seasonless clothing that can be worn most or all of the year. Much of today's sportswear is designed to combine easily and to work well in layers. Any garment that meets these two requirements is a good all-year-round choice.

Seasonless clothing should function as the backbone of any wardrobe. Unlined corduroy slacks, for example, can be worn in all but below-zero weather, and they can even be worn then if your child is wearing tights, long underwear, or leg warmers. Short-sleeve polo shirts are a good buy for all seasons: when the warm weather is over, they can be worn under sweaters for additional warmth. Light-weight turtlenecks can be worn alone in the fall and spring and, in cold climates, underneath shirts in the winter. Try to buy seasonless clothes: these items normally provide the most wearings for your money.

THE CLOTHING EFFICIENCY FORMULA

The true cost of an article of clothing is not the price on the tag, but the *cost per wearing*—the amount of money you wind up spending each time your child actually puts the piece of clothing on. The more times your child wears an item before it is outgrown, given away, or worn out, the lower the cost per wearing. Sometimes a seemingly expensive garment can be cheaper in the long run than a sale item at half the price. For example, a pair of very dressy slacks purchased at $20 and worn six times in two years (to church and to a wedding) costs far more per wearing than less dressy but still stylish slacks purchased at the higher price of $25 but worn thirty times (to both school and formal occasions).

Generally, the clothes that will have the lowest cost per wearing are those that fit into the general categories we have already outlined:

1. Clothes that are classically styled and that are likely to remain in fashion for years
2. Items that can be worn most or all of the year, either separately or matched or layered with other items
3. Apparel that can function in a variety of settings and situations
4. Clothing that is well made, durable, and generally of high quality

White knits by Norma Kamali are eye-catching for spring, summer, or fall.

Our Clothing Efficiency Formula will tell you how much of a bargain a particular article of clothing is for you. The result of the formula is the estimated *cost per wearing* of a garment: the lower the cost per wearing, the better a buy the item is for you.

You don't need to use the Clothing Efficiency Formula until you've found an item of clothing that you think you may want to buy. Don't worry about the price of an item at first. Let your child try on everything you both like, regardless of the price. Unless the price is truly ridiculous, the garment could conceivably turn out to have a relatively small cost per wearing.

The Clothing Efficiency Formula looks like this:

$$\frac{\text{Cost of an item}}{\text{Estimated number of times the item will be worn}} = \text{Cost per wearing}$$

Simply divide the cost of the item by the estimated number of times the garment will be worn. This provides you with the *cost of the item per wearing*. Obviously, the cheaper the price per wearing, the better a bargain that article of clothing is for you, *regardless of the price on the price tag*.

Let's look at a couple of examples:

Michelle is an eleven-year-old girl whose mother has bought her a gray flannel blazer and a sundress. The blazer cost Michelle's mom $50. She estimates that it will be worn to school (with jeans, with slacks, and with skirts); as a fall and spring jacket; and in the winter under Michelle's heavy coat. The blazer will be too heavy to wear in the summer, however.

Michelle's mother calculates that Michelle will wear the blazer about twice a week for nine months of the year, and that it will fit Michelle for about two years. This works out to 160 wearings (*40 weeks per year* × *2 wearings per week* × *2 years*). For the blazer, the Clothing Efficiency Formula would look like this:

$$\frac{\$50.00}{160 \text{ Wearings}} = \$0.3125 = 31.25 \text{ cents per wearing}$$

At less than 32 cents per wearing, we can see that the blazer is well worth the price.

Now let's look at the sundress. Michelle's mother bought it on sale (reduced from \$30 to \$18). She did not apply the Clothing Efficiency Formula before buying the dress because at the time it seemed like a bargain. It's a fairly dressy sundress, perfect for outdoor parties.

Because Michelle and her family live in Chicago, the weather is warm enough for the sundress only about four months of the year. It is too nice for playing in, however, and so it winds up getting worn only during family outings, social occasions, and so on. It fits Michelle for two summers and gets worn perhaps twelve times each summer.

Let's apply the Clothing Efficiency Formula:

$$\frac{\$18.00}{24 \text{ Wearings}} = \$0.75 = 75 \text{ cents per wearing}$$

Clearly, this sundress was not as much of a bargain as the blazer.

The better you are genuinely able to estimate the actual number of times your child will wear an article of clothing, the better the Clothing Efficiency Formula will work for you. As you use the formula over the weeks, months, and years (and as you get more familiar with what your child will wear and won't wear), you will get better at making these estimates.

Remember, the key questions you need to ask yourself about the true cost of an item of apparel are the following:

1. How long will the item stay in fashion?
2. How much of the year can it be worn?
3. How well does it fit with other items in your child's wardrobe?
4. Can it be worn in a variety of settings and situations?

In the store, of course, you are only estimating the cost per wearing. The actual cost per wearing is determined by the number of times your child actually puts the item on. This means the Clothing Efficiency Formula will work for you only if you are honest and reasonable about the projected number of times your child will wear something. Do not overestimate simply because you like a piece of clothing very much; the actual cost per wearing will not change because of wishful thinking.

Now you are ready to go shopping.

12

The Fine Art of Shopping

U P UNTIL NOW WE HAVE GIVEN you all kinds of information about colors, styles, fabrics, quality, kids' personalities, and so on. Now it is your turn to put it all into practice by actually going shopping.

If you take the following steps, shopping for your child's clothing will go most smoothly, efficiently, and successfully. First, make sure you know exactly what items you want to buy for your child. This can be done either formally or informally. An inventory is not always necessary, of course. If your daughter has ruined her Girl Scout blouse, you obviously do not need to inventory her wardrobe to figure out that she needs this blouse replaced. Use your common sense in determining when to look through your child's wardrobe and when to work from memory.

When you know what your child needs, boil that list down into what you actually intend to buy on this particular trip. You might be buying everything he or she needs or only one or two of those items. You might want to make two or more trips, purchasing only a few items each time. Don't try to do too much on one trip! Shopping can be exhausting for adults and children alike, and trying to do too much can make you or your child— or both of you—angry and irritable. Remember, your child will be going shopping with you, and a child's patience and attention span are usually quite a bit shorter than an adult's. Don't try to

drag your son or daughter from store to store for more than about two hours. Any longer than that and he or she is probably going to get mighty cranky. One way to avoid this is to shop for a while, take a break or have lunch or see a movie, and then shop a while longer.

It is important that you consult with your child in advance about any shopping trip. Shopping for clothes is one of the few things that can be done just as well on Thursday as on Saturday, and new clothes are rarely an absolutely immediate need. So every shopping trip should be planned around both of your schedules. Don't make your son miss playing shortstop in a Little League game because you want to get him some new pajamas. This Little League game will only happen once; pajamas will still be available next week.

When making up your list of what you are going to buy, be sure to include the following information *for each item*:

1. The name of the item (socks, blouses, scarf, and so forth)
2. The size your child wears for each item
3. Any particular brand names, styles, or designs that you feel look especially good on your child or that your child has asked for in the past
4. Any preferences for the kind of fabric in a garment
5. Any preferences for color. Keep your child's basic color and second color in mind. Also keep in mind the colors of items in his or her wardrobe that might go with whatever you are planning to buy.
6. Any notes to yourself about what looks good on your child: stripes, rows of buttons, light colors, and so forth
7. Put your child's measurements for neck, chest, waist, hips, and leg inseam on the bottom of your list. You never know when you will need them.
8. It is also helpful to list exactly the stores you will be going to and directions, in order to simplify your shopping. Planning this out in advance can save you time, anxiety, and even a few dollars on gas.

After you've made up your list, it's a good idea to discuss it with your children before setting out for the stores. Tell them what you plan to buy; find out what they would like to see on the list. Encourage them to be specific about colors and styles. If your ideas differ, work out a compromise. These discussions work best if you sit down with only one child at a time. This allows each child to speak freely, without fear of interference or of causing jealousy. It's also just plain quieter, calmer, and simpler for you. Best of all, it avoids arguments among children.

Although busy parents may wonder if they'll actually be able to take time out for these pre-shopping-trip huddles with their kids, we strongly feel that it's worth making the attempt. By doing so, you and your children know exactly what you're going to buy before you leave home. Even better, you each agree on what you're going to buy! This saves everyone time and prevents arguments and hassle.

Now you are ready to head for the stores! Don't forget to bring these items with you:

- The list you have just made up
- A tape measure, just in case
- Your completed Inventory Form. You never know when this might be helpful
- This book, for reference

SHOPPING TIPS

Here are some tips that will make shopping for your child's clothes more pleasant and productive.

1. Bring your child with you when you go shopping for his or her clothes. It's much easier to have your child try something on than to have to run back to the store to return an item.
2. If at all possible, take only one child shopping at a time.
3. Know exactly where you are going to shop before you leave the house. Have a second or third store in mind in case the first one does not have what you want.
4. Don't be distracted by other stores or by other items or departments in the same store. You can buy yourself dresses, blenders, and new tires some other time. Distractions can be a waste of time, they can cause you to spend more money than you can afford, and they can make your child grumpy or angry.
5. Remember to think in terms of what looks terrific on *your* child. An adorable mannequin wearing gorgeous

trendy clothes may look a great deal better than your child will in those same clothes. And your child, wearing a very different outfit, may look far more attractive than that mannequin ever will.

6. It is worth the small amount of time, money, and effort to glance at some current fashion magazines or store catalogs before going shopping, just to get a general idea of what is in and coming into style. Let your child look at these magazines, too, and have him or her point out items that he or she likes.

7. Encourage your youngster to stay by your side while you are shopping. There is nothing more aggravating than having him or her disappear and having to spend twenty minutes hunting for him.

8. Before you leave the house, make sure that your child is appropriately dressed for trying on the kinds of clothing you will be looking at. Shoes should be easy to get off and on. If you are going to look at pants, have him or her wear pants rather than overalls or a dress.

9. Also, a little check-up for clean face and hands isn't a bad idea. It's a small matter, but kids who look like they've just come off a rough day at the playground aren't going to look too hot in most of the clothes they try on.

10. Give your child directions on what to do if he or she gets lost or if you are separated from each other. Your best bet is to pick a spot in each store (the front door or a particular department or counter works well) and to arrange to meet there if something happens.

11. Remember that strollers are not permitted on escalators.

12. Make sure your children understand that they are not to put merchandise in their pockets, nor are they to take something with them from one department and carry it to another. Young children often do not understand the concept of purchasing things—or the concept of theft. It can be embarrassing to you (and frightening to your child) if he or she is stopped by the store detective, even if it is obvious to everyone that he or she meant no harm.

13. From the time your child is old enough to understand money, explain how the process of purchasing things works. Show him or her the price tag, and your money, checkbook, or charge card. Explain what is happening

when your purchases are being rung up and when you are handing over money, writing a check, or using your credit card. This will help teach your child the value and use of money.

14. After you have been shopping for a while—or when your child looks like he or she is starting to get cranky or tired—take a break. Sit down somewhere and relax. Parks and snack bars are good spots. Have something to eat or drink, and use this time to just talk or play with your child. This will provide a welcome break, and when it is over, you should both be feeling good and ready to shop some more.

15. If your child is tired, hungry, or in a bad mood, do not take him or her shopping unless you can make him or her feel better first. Otherwise your child is likely to be uncooperative at best, and impossible at worst. If your child is tired, let him or her take a nap first. If your youngster is hungry, fix him or her something to eat.

16. Always treat shopping as a fun activity, not as a chore that you must force yourself through. This way your child will look at shopping as something positive from a very young age.

17. Younger children will often do better on shopping trips if you let them bring one of their favorite toys with them.

Children as young as two can have definite likes and dislikes in clothing, especially when it comes to color. So allow your child to express preferences in clothing from a very small age, and listen to them. From the age of two or three, your child should be helping you make clothing decisions.

As your children grow older, they can take an increasingly larger share of responsibilities in choosing their clothing. By the time children are about twelve, they should be able to make most or all of their own selections of clothing, relying on you for guidance only. However, the degree of independence you allow your children should be based on their maturity, not on their age.

Use shopping trips as opportunities to help teach your child the principles of kids' chic. As a young child tries items on, explain to him or her about colors and designs. As your son or daughter grows older you can talk to him or her about fabrics, putting outfits together, wardrobes, and so on. Don't try to explain too much at once, and don't turn your shopping trips into lectures.

You are buying your children the clothes they genuinely need, and sometimes one child will simply need more clothing than another. So don't feel guilty about this apparent "unfairness"—and don't feel you need to balance every purchase for one son or daughter with a little something for the others. If a child complains, simply explain why you're doing what you're doing and tell him or her that you trust he or she is grown up enough to understand.

The special item your child wants so badly and that you have agreed to get should be the *last* thing you buy on your shopping trip. This helps assure you of your child's cooperation throughout your trip.

SHOPPING OPTIONS

Parents today have more ways and places to shop for their kids' clothes than ever before. We have listed below the most popular retail shopping options and the pros and cons of each. We will describe in detail over a dozen different discount shopping options in Chapter 13.

DEPARTMENT STORES. These stores feature a large stock of well-organized and attractively presented merchandise. Although there can be great variation from one store to another, or even within the same store, department stores usually sell medium to high-quality clothing. Department stores' prices tend to be moderate to high (depending on the particular store), though sale prices are often quite reasonable.

Department stores offer the widest range of services. These can include gift wrapping, baby-sitting, special programs for children such as storytelling and puppet shows, layaways, alterations, and personal shopping consultants who will suggest particular purchases and help you plan your child's wardrobe. Dayton's in Minneapolis offers a computerized gift registry in its children's department. Called The Stork Club, this baby registry provides gift givers with a computer printout just like a bridal registry. This printout contains a list of items you would enjoy receiving as gifts for your baby. Gift information is kept on the computer from the time your baby is born until her or his second birthday.

According to the *Wall Street Journal*, among the department stores, The J.C. Penney Co. and Sears have been leaders in children's wear for many years, selling their store-brand outfits at moderate prices. Big department stores, such as Macy's and Bloomingdales, feature the more expensive labels and serve an upscale market.

CHILDREN'S SPECIALTY STORES. These stores specialize either in children's clothing and accessories or in clothing and other children's items (toys, bedding, cribs, etc.). Some stores specialize in products for infants and toddlers.

The salespeople in children's specialty stores are usually well informed and well trained, and these stores often offer an array of customer services, including charge accounts, returns, delivery, gift wrapping, layaways, and alterations. Their best feature is personal shopping assistance and advice. If you can get to know the owner or salespeople at a particular store, you can often get them to order special items for you or to let you know when a particularly great buy comes in. Because the children's wear business is currently enjoying an unprecedented boom, children's specialty boutiques are popping up in large numbers in cities all around the country.

Prices at children's specialty stores range from moderate to high, sometimes *very* high. The hours of children's specialty stores are usually not as long as those of department stores.

CATALOG SALES. Shopping by catalog has come a long way since Sears's first *Wish Book* came out in 1895. Catalog shopping has the advantages of saving time, being more convenient, and being fun in many ways. You can pick out products in your own home or you and your child can pick them out together. And where else can you shop at 1:00 A.M., when it's quiet and peaceful?

Today, the catalogs themselves are of very high quality, and their photographs show accurate colors and details. Depending on what you are looking for, you can order catalogs for discount merchandise, retail merchandise, imported items, high-fashion and designer clothing, and special items.

Most catalog enterprises require you to order by mail, but some have stores where you can place your order in person. You can then either pick your order up at the store when it arrives or have it sent directly to your home. Some of these stores have a large selection of items already in stock.

Catalog stores often have sales just as department stores do, and most of them offer a full refund for returns. Not all do, however, so be careful. Many catalog stores will send gifts, already boxed or wrapped, directly to the recipient. Often a card can be included.

Some catalog stores sell virtually anything. Others specialize in apparel for both adults and children. A few specialize in items for children, either in clothes and accessories alone, or in clothes, accessories, toys, and other children's items.

The following companies specialize in children's wear:

> Great American Kids' Clothes
> 600 West 58th Street
> Department 9019
> New York, New York 10019

Brochures cost $1 and display classic, functional clothes such as Shetland sweaters, corduroy pants, lumber jackets, oxford-cloth shirts, denim jeans, and coveralls.

> Kids Warehouse
> Brownell Hollow Road
> Eagle Bridge, New York 12057

This company focuses on country clothes in natural fabrics. They charge $1 for a year's subscription of six brochures.

> Pure Kid
> 189 Huntington Street
> Carroll Gardens, New York 11231

The Pure Kid Catalog costs $2 per issue. Pure Kid is a good source of cotton clothing for younger children up to size 4. It includes items from many well-known manufacturers.

The big drawback of catalog sales is obvious: your child cannot try any item on before you buy it. So, convenient as catalog shopping may be, you may find yourself returning some items.

Some useful tips in catalog shopping include:

1. If you are unfamiliar with the company, investigate to make sure it is legitimate. Good places to begin are the Better Business Bureau and the Chamber of Commerce. Be wary of mail-order companies that only list a post office box number.
2. Note the company's policy on returns. If they don't accept returns, don't order anything. If they accept exchanges but not returns, they are still best avoided. You might not like what you ordered and might also not like anything else enough to want to make the exchange. Also, pay attention to time limitations on returns. Thirty days is reasonable; anything less may prove inconvenient.
3. Look at delivery dates. If it's close to a holiday, check guaranteed delivery dates. If you need the item by a certain time and the company doesn't guarantee delivery on or before that date, don't use that company. If no dates are specified, call and ask for their guaranteed delivery times.
4. Keep a record of each order, including the following information: name of item, color, size; company's name, address, phone number; date of order; and any special instructions. Keep all records and correspondence together in a convenient, easily accessible place.
5. If any key information is absent in the ad or order blank (sizes or colors available, dimensions, etc.) be sure to specify your desires or call or write a query first.
6. If you need the item soon, think again before ordering by mail.
7. If you don't receive the service you desire, notify the Mail Order Action Line Service:

> Mail Order Action Line
> c/o Direct Mail/Marketing Associates
> 6 East 43rd Street
> New York, New York 10017
> (212) 689–4977

SALES AND COUPONS

When good clothes that your child needs are on sale, try to buy. Watch the newspapers for ads that tell of current or upcoming sales. Look for discount coupons in newspapers, local magazines, community newspapers, advertising supplements, TV guides, fliers, and so on. If you see a coupon that you might be able to use, cut it and save it. Don't forget to bring it with you when you shop. These coupons can save you a lot of money: a 20 percent coupon to a high-quality clothing store can make a big difference.

As you enter a department or discount store, look at the bulletin boards or signs near the entrance. Usually a copy of the store's current ad will be on display. Scan this ad to see what bargains are available.

Here is a list of common sales and when they take place:

Bargain Calendar

Month	Description/Items
January	After Christmas sales. Children's wear—good bargains for winterwear and winter sports clothing and equipment. Bedding, toys, bicycles, and small appliances like radios and phonographs are usually on sale.
February	Final markdowns on winter clothes. Presidents' Day storewide sale.
March	Early spring sale. Legwear such as socks, tights, leg warmers. Underwear, children's shoes.
April	After Easter general storewide sales. Children's coats and jackets. Sleepwear, boys' suits, and girls' dresses. Preseason summer camp and sporting equipment.
May	Memorial Day general store sales. Early summer promotions.
June	Boys' clothing. Spring sales around Father's Day.
July	July 4th sales on summer merchandise, including children's clothing, sportswear, shoes, accessories.
August	Back-to-school specials. Final markdowns on summer clothes. Preseason sales on coats and boots.
September	Back-to-school general sale. Special sales after Labor Day.
October	Sale on school clothes. Coat sale. Columbus Day general sale.
November	Veterans Day general sales. Thanksgiving begins major Christmas push with selected specials.
December	Pre- and post-Christmas general merchandise sales.

Here are a few important terms you should know when shopping sales:

Comparable value. Indicates that an item is quite similar to a competitor's product that is sold at a higher price. For example, if Macy's sells Brand X jeans at $15 and Gimbels sells Brand Y jeans at $20, Macy's might advertise Brand X jeans by saying, "Comparable value, $20. Now only $15."

Introductory offer. An initial sale of a new product, in an attempt to get you to try that product. These offers are usually real: after a few days or weeks, the price on that item will probably rise to its "normal" selling price.

Irregulars. Garments with slight flaws that may or may not be noticeable but that are sold at major discounts.

Seconds. Items of apparel with flaws worse than those of irregulars.

Suggested retail price. The manufacturer's official suggested price for a garment or other item. It is usually about twice the wholesale price. Most clothing can be purchased below this price with a little patience and shopping around.

13

Cheap Chic

THERE ARE NO TWO WAYS ABOUT it: children's clothes are expensive. While it would be wonderful if we could afford a complete wardrobe of brand-new, top-quality clothing for each of our children, this is not often possible. Some parents need to cut a few corners when it comes to buying clothes for their kids. This chapter will show you how to save money without giving up style. We'll start off by looking at used clothing. Getting special buys on new clothing will be discussed later in this chapter.

Some parents feel guilty about buying used clothing for their children or making a younger child wear hand-me-downs. Don't. Almost all parents take advantage of used clothes. Some children are unhappy or embarrassed at not having brand-new clothes to wear, especially if their friends have new clothes. It's true that secondhand clothing will probably not be the most exciting part of a youngster's wardrobe (unless there's a long-envied item in the older sibling's closet that the younger boy or girl is itching to possess). Part of the problem is the "take what you get" aspect of used clothes. Kids in particular enjoy picking out their own things, especially the things they wear. So if you're using hand-me-downs in an outfit, we recommend that you blend them with clothes that you and your child bought yourselves. Or make the outfit special and personal with attention-getting belts, pins, or legwear.

For a friend of ours who buys secondhand clothing regularly, the "take what you get" aspect is never a problem. For years, the family struggled along on an income that varied from year to year. So she made a virtue out of necessity and turned shopping at garage sales and secondhand stores a hobby and an art. Her local newspaper lists weekend garage sales in the community, and she'll set off early on Saturday morning, even if she only has half an hour to spare. This woman always seems to find *great-looking* used outfits to wear herself—which she carries off beautifully—and her own excitement about her "finds" rubs off on her children. They've grown up with cheap chic and will probably practice it with ease and know-how when they reach adulthood.

Never skimp on fit, style, comfort, or appearance in used clothing. You wouldn't buy a used car that was missing a carburetor. Why should you buy less than attractive or less than comfortable clothing for your child? Secondhand should never be second-rate.

The same rules apply to hand-me-downs as to used clothing. If an older sister outgrows a dress, that dress should be added to your younger daughter's wardrobe only if it passes all the Kids' Chic tests. It makes no difference that the dress still looks pretty if your younger child hates it or feels uncomfortable in it. It also makes no difference that you spent good money on it—after all, you didn't buy it for your younger daughter.

HAND-ME-DOWNS

Almost every child has at least some hand-me-down clothing. The big problem with hand-me-downs is that they make your child's wardrobe far less unified and cohesive than if you were to go out and buy all his or her clothing new. For example, Kimmel might look best in blue, and this has been her basic color for a few years. However, her older sister Becky looks best in yellow, so many of Becky's old clothes are yellow. When these are handed down to Kimmel, they simply do not look as good on her as they did on her older sister.

The key to making hand-me-downs work is simply to put them through the same tests we've outlined for new clothing. Is the color a flattering one? If you're building a wardrobe around one color, as we suggest in Chapter 1, you'll have to figure out if the item in question can fit into your scheme. But if there are clothes in the used pile that your youngster is clearly unexcited about, don't force them on him or her.

Although some parents are lucky enough to have children who are only a size or two apart from one another, usually an older child grows out of his or her clothes years before the next child is big enough to wear them. This means having to store hand-me-downs for a few years. For storing clothing, proper care and organization are important. The best method for storage is to sort all the clothing according to item, size, and season. Then store everything in small cartons, with each carton clearly marked according to item, size, and season. Make sure each carton is closed tightly so that moths and dust cannot get in. If a hand-me-down needs repairing or if it has a stain that needs to be removed, take care of this before storing it. See Chapter 14 for information on stain removal.

BUYING USED CLOTHING

Buying used clothing can save you money, but shopping for it almost always takes a great deal more time. For many busy parents, time is their scantiest commodity. However, if you can afford to take the time to shop carefully and to remove stains or make repairs when necessary, used clothing may be a real bargain.

Remember that buying used clothing is hardly ever as easy as buying new clothes. Garments are not as well organized in the store, and it is always a gamble whether any store, rummage sale, or flea market will have anything you can use. So be patient and persistent when looking for used bargains.

Used clothing can be purchased at any of the following:

THRIFT STORES. Thrift stores can be found in almost any community. Some are privately run, but many are part of large national chains such as Goodwill, St. Vincent dePaul, and the Salvation Army. These are the places to go to get clothes at very cheap prices.

Some thrift stores simply pile their clothes in bins, but most have their items displayed on racks. However, items are not usually grouped together by size, so you must look through a great many garments to find the right size.

You can often find surprisingly high quality items at very low prices in thrift stores—cashmere sweaters for $10, wool jackets for $2, or plain slacks for less than a dollar. However, the quality of clothing can vary widely within the same store. In short, you never know what you will find.

VINTAGE CLOTHING STORES. Vintage clothing stores sell high-quality used clothing. Often this clothing is old or "antique," but it has remained in style or has come back into style. Sometimes vintage clothing stores also have a selection of regular used clothing as well. Prices in these stores are usually a good deal higher than those in thrift shops; they average about 30 percent to 65 percent of the price of similar new items. Usually the clothing sold at vintage clothing stores is in excellent condition and fairly attractively displayed. However, some vintage clothing stores do not have much of a selection for children.

CONSIGNMENT SHOPS. Consignment shops, also called resale stores, usually sell high-quality used clothing for adults and children. Some sell new (and even handmade) clothing as well. Consignment shops normally accept and sell only clothing that is in good or excellent condition—free of holes, tears, and stains, and with plenty of potential use still left. Usually, anyone can bring in used clothing to a consignment shop; if it's in good enough condition, the shop accepts and prices it, and puts it up for sale in the store for about ninety days. If the item sells within that time, the store splits the money with the person who brought in the garment, usually 50/50. If the garment is not sold within ninety days, it is returned to its original owner.

Consignment shops are usually good places to find quality children's clothing at good prices. Prices tend to be higher than at thrift stores, but only about 50 percent of what you would pay for those same items new. Get to know the staffs of resale shops in your area. Find out from them when they put out newly arrived clothing. If you become a regular customer, you can often get one of them to call you when a particular article arrives that you are looking for. Consignment stores are also a good place for you to bring clothing that your own children have outgrown.

GARAGE AND RUMMAGE SALES. Garage and rummage sales are by far the most unpredictable places to shop for your child's clothing, but they can be the most fun. You can find gorgeous, well-made items at ridiculously low prices; or you can spend all day and find nothing at all.

Because rummage sales are run by people who are not professional, you never know what the prices will be at any sale. Usually, though, items are priced very low so that their owners can get rid of them. And more often than not, you can haggle over the price of *almost anything.*

We've seen rummage sales where clothing was ordered by sizes and hung carefully on racks, and others where it was just piled in boxes. We've seen prices of five cents and ten cents for shirts, pants, and skirts, and prices of $5 and $10 for fairly similar items.

Rummage sales are often run by organizations (churches, schools, neighborhood associations, etc.). In sales of this type, many people donate items for a large sale to be held under one roof, and you will find a huge variety of merchandise available in one place. The best times to go to rummage and garage sales are either when they first open up on their first day or when they are just about to close down on their last day. Getting there for the opening assures you of the widest choice of items. Often the cream of a rummage sale gets skimmed off within the first half hour or even the first few minutes. Getting there at the very end of the sale leaves you with the smallest choice, but you can often find some outrageous bargains. The people running the sale want to get rid of what they have left, and they know that they have almost no time left to do it. Forget the price tags on items at this point, and make some offers. Offer a quarter or a third of what's written on the tag.

Rummage and garage sales are often announced in the classified ads of newspapers, especially neighborhood newspapers. Also look for signs on bulletin boards, telephone poles, and front lawns.

TIPS FOR BUYING USED CLOTHING

1. Finding a fitting room may be hard, especially at rummage and garage sales. Always ask if such a spot is available.

2. Remember to look over each item carefully. Is it genuinely usable? Does it really fit into your child's wardrobe or does it at least fit with a couple of items in it?
3. Do not overbuy. This is very easy to do, so very consciously avoid it. Do not get your child anything she or he doesn't need.
4. It can often take months to complete a child's wardrobe when you are buying primarily or entirely used clothing. Therefore, preplanning and patience are essential.
5. Knowing exactly what you want to buy is every bit as essential when shopping for used clothing as it is when you are buying new items. Make a list and bring it with you, together with your child's measurements.

CHECKING THE CONDITION
OF USED CLOTHING

In addition to checking garments for fit, feel, color, comfort, and all the other factors we have already discussed, you will need to check used clothing carefully to see that it is in wearable—or at least repairable—condition. Here is a checklist to use when shopping for used clothing for your child:

Inspection Checklist for Used Clothing

Inspection Points	Comments
Stains and spots	If fiber content is 100 percent natural, there is a possibility of removing the stain. If the fiber is synthetic or a blend, the stains are probably permanent. If you are not sure of the fiber content, don't buy the garment.
Buttons	Are they there? These can usually be replaced easily.
Hems	Check for intact hem; frayed cuffs can be shortened; hemline marks do not come out.
Zippers	Do they work? (Ability to replace depends on the type of zipper.)
Seams	Check for rips, especially in stress areas such as seat, crotch, armholes, etc. If a seam is torn, don't buy the item.
Holes and tears	Evaluate each for the possibility of patching or repairing.

Inspection Points	Comments
Pilling on sweater and shirts	These garments are of questionable value.
Quilted or down-filled garments	If the inner filling has shifted, don't buy the item.
Seat and crotch	Don't buy if worn out.
Elbows on shirts and sweaters; knees on pants	Don't buy if too thin.
Pockets	Ripped pockets are easily repairable.
Linings	Check for rips. May have to be replaced if damaged.
Straps	Easy to repair if torn.

MORE CHEAP CHIC

Here are some other places and situations where you can save money on new and used clothing for your child:

Bazaar. A bazaar is a gathering of individuals who sell items, often at a regular place and time, in an informal setup such as a marketplace or fair. Bazaars usually sell used items, but sometimes new items are available, too. Bartering, swapping, and low prices are common. Use the same techniques and tips here as you would for rummage sales. No returns. Also called *flea markets*.

Clearance sale. Goods are offered at lower prices in order to clear out a store's shelves for the next season. Traditionally these are mostly end-of-the-season or out-of-season goods. Sometimes returns are accepted, sometimes not.

Close-out sale. Discontinued products or out-of-season items are offered by retailers at a savings. Pickings are sometimes slim, but the values can be large. Usually no returns are permitted.

Close-out store. A close-out store may also be called a *liquidation store* or *liquidation outlet*. This store offers one-time-only merchandise, usually at low prices. It can do this by buying large lots of discontinued merchandise from retailers trying to liquidate because of bankruptcy, fires, floods, or insurance company directions. The kinds of items available in a close-out store can vary greatly from one week to the next. Cash and carry. No services, returns, or charges.

Designer discount stores. This type of retailer offers high-quality, famous-label clothing at special savings. Frequently the labels have been removed, but otherwise the merchandise is new and authentic. Returns are normally permitted. Right now the off-price market is booming, as more and more consumers are discovering that they can get brand-new designer clothing at substantial discounts. The most notable entrant into this market is Kids 'R Us, a division of the highly successful Toys 'R Us Corporation. As reported in both the *New York Times* and the *Wall Street Journal*, the arrival of Kids 'R Us caused reverberations throughout the industry, as established department stores and children's clothing chains braced for the competition. What distinguishes Kids 'R Us from other discount chains is their size, their huge selection of clothing and accessories, and their colorful and appealing decor. While many discount stores have a plain, bargain-basement look, the two pilot Kids 'R Us stores look like playlands, complete with fun-house mirrors and huge stuffed animals for kids to play on. Although only two stores exist at present—one in Brooklyn, New York, and one in New Jersey—both the Toys 'R Us Corporation and the rest of the industry are watching these very closely.

Discount store. This is a store operating on a low margin of markup. It is usually self-service. Sometimes this store offers high-quality or stylish merchandise at substantial savings. Returns are usually accepted. Marshalls is a coast-to-coast discount chain.

Estate sales. This is a sale of an entire family's belongings. An estate sale is usually run by professional appraisers, often after a death in a family. A great source for antique items and excellent (and often vintage) used clothing. Often a pirate's bounty. No returns, of course.

Flea markets. See Bazaars.

Government surplus store. This type of store buys military surplus and other merchandise and sells it to civilians at a considerable savings. This store sells all sorts of items from utility clothing to camping items. Returns are usually OK.

Liquidation stores. See Close-out store.

Mass merchandiser. Mass merchandisers are chains of stores featuring low-priced goods that are popular to large numbers of people. Some of these stores are essentially department stores offering a wide variety of items, from clothing to plants to automobile tires. Others specialize just in clothing. K Mart and Shopco are examples. Mass merchandisers emphasize low prices and high values, plus a large selection. Although these stores may not be noted for their fashion leadership, they do offer clothing that is basically popular at low to moderate prices. However, the quality of clothing offered at these stores can range from very low to quite high, so be careful. Most of these stores offer charge accounts, and most allow returns and exchanges on almost every item. Mass merchandisers regularly have specials and sales. Seasonal markdowns can be good buys in all categories. Most mass merchandisers offer few services. Gift wrapping is not usually available; delivery is almost never available. Help from salespeople is much harder to get than at higher-priced stores, and the salespeople are much less knowledgeable and much more informal. Most mass merchandisers are open ten to twelve hours a day, usually seven days a week. These stores are good places to buy fad items at relatively low prices.

Outlet store. An outlet store is run by a manufacturer and is located either by a main warehouse or by factories where the manufacturing is done. These stores sell regular merchandise, items that have been overproduced, irregulars, seconds, samples, and/or discontinued items or styles—all at very low prices. They may also sell trim accessories or wholesale fabric. Usually specializing in one particular line of clothing, outlet stores are becoming very popular. In some areas, several of these outlet stores are located together in one shopping center. Check your Yellow Pages to find the clothing manufacturers in your area; call to see which ones have outlet stores. These stores are beginning to do limited advertising, particularly for their end-of-season sales. Returns are sometimes (but not often) permitted at these stores. Also called *factory outlets* and *manufacturer's outlets*.

Sample shop. A sample shop sells new clothes inexpensively. Some sample stores sell only children's clothing; others sell clothing for both children and adults. In these shops, sales representatives sell off their stock as well as manufacturer's overruns and seasonal leftovers. Returns and exchanges are usually difficult here, if they are accepted at all. Seasonal sample sales may also be held in people's homes, hotels, or sales representatives' offices. A limited range of sizes is usually available.

Special purchases. By special arrangement with a manufacturer, a store offers special savings and reduced prices on particular items. The store buys the item at a cut price, then passes the discount directly on to the customer in one of three ways: (1) as part of a special sale; (2) as part of their regular stock; or (3) by selling irregulars. Returns are usually OK.

Warehouse sales. These offer special savings for customers who shop for goods at a warehouse location rather than at the company's retail store. Returns are normally permitted, and usually these items can be charged.

While researching this book, we've found that many parents are finding that the savings offered in discount outlets are just too attractive to resist. While they realize that in many of these stores a high percentage of the merchandise is of mediocre or poor quality, they're becoming more and more willing to search out the "treasures." One mother became convinced when she found a $28 pair of Yves Saint Laurent knickers at Marshalls for $14. "That was it," she declares. "I just don't pay full price for anything anymore."

Part V

Taking Care

14

Clothing Maintenance

TO GET THE MOST OUT OF ANY garment or accessory, it must not only be purchased wisely, it must be taken care of properly. A garment that is not well cared for is not likely to look as good or last as long as one that has been properly looked after.

It is extremely important that you follow the washing and drying instructions on the label of any item of clothing. Never remove this label! It is your key to the garment's proper care.

We have reprinted a chart prepared by the American Apparel Manufacturers Association that explains in detail all the terms used on clothing labels.

STAINS

Any garment that becomes soiled or stained looks unattractive no matter how fashionable or expensive it is. However, it is anything but economical to throw away a garment when it becomes soiled or stained. If something does get stained, try to remove the stain *immediately*, if at all possible. If not, remove it as soon as you can. The longer you wait, the longer the stain has a chance to set.

The following information will be useful in helping you remove most kinds of stains from virtually any fabric. It has been reprinted with the permission of The Maytag Company.

Consumer Care Guide for Apparel

Basic Labels	Meaning
Washable Machine Washable Machine Wash	Wash, bleach, dry, and press by any customary method including commercial laundering.
Home launder only	Same as above but do not use commercial laundering.
No bleach	Do not use bleach.
No starch	Do not use starch.
Cold wash Cold setting Cold rinse	Use cold water from tap or cold washing-machine setting.
Warm wash Warm setting Warm rinse	Use warm water: 90° to 110° Fahrenheit.
Hot wash Hot setting	Use hot water (hot washing-machine setting): 130° Fahrenheit or hotter.
No spin	Remove wash load before final machine spin cycle.
Delicate cycle Gentle cycle	Use appropriate machine setting; otherwise wash by hand.
Durable press cycle Permanent press cycle	Use appropriate machine setting; otherwise use medium wash, cold rinse, and short spin cycle.
Wash separately	Wash alone or with like colors
Hand washable Hand-wash	Launder only by hand in lukewarm (hand-comfortable) water. May be bleached. May be dry-cleaned.
Hand-wash only	Same as above, but do not dry-clean.
Hand-wash separately	Hand-wash alone or with like colors.

Basic Labels	Meaning
Tumble dry Machine dry	Dry in tumble dryer at specified setting: high, medium, low or no heat.
Tumble dry Remove promptly	Same as above, but in absence of cool-down cycle, remove at once when tumbling stops.
Drip dry Hang dry Line dry	Hang wet and allow to dry with hand-shaping only.
No squeeze No wring No twist	Hang dry, drip dry, or dry flat only.
Dry flat	Lay garment on flat surface.
Block to dry	Maintain original size and shape while drying.
Cool iron	Set iron at lowest setting.
Warm iron	Set iron at medium setting.
Hot iron	Set iron at hot setting.
No iron No press	Do not iron or press with heat.
Steam iron Steam press	Iron or press with steam.
Iron damp	Dampen garment before ironing.
Dry-clean Dry-clean only	Garment should be dry-cleaned only, including self-service.
Professionally clean only Commercially clean only	Do not use self-service dry cleaning.
No dry-clean	Use recommended care instructions. No dry-cleaning materials to be used.

GARMENT SAVING GUIDELINES

Stain removal doesn't have to be complicated—and it doesn't require a shelf full of drugstore supplies. Three out of four common stains can be simply removed by presoaking or pretreating and then laundering in hot water with chlorine bleach.

The "Three P's" of Stain Removal

Some stains are stubborn and require a little extra effort. But most stains can eventually be removed or at least lightened by following these guidelines:

PROMPTNESS: Very important! Treat stains as quickly as possible before laundering. Aging and laundering before pretreatment can set some stains.

PATIENCE: If the garment is worth saving, it is worth a little extra time and effort to follow stain removal procedures.

PERSEVERANCE: Some stains are difficult to remove. It may be necessary to repeat a procedure several times before a stain is removed.

Some stains are impossible to remove and some can only be lightened even after following the most elaborate stain removal procedure.

Refer to the chart on the following pages for recommended procedures.

Elements for Successful Stain Removal

Soaking:

Some stains require soaking before further treatment—some in cold water, some in warm or hot water. Enzyme presoaks can be used according to manufacturer's instructions for removing certain stains. FABRIC PRECAUTION: Sort carefully and avoid soaking for an excessively long time. Dyes in some fabrics are unstable and may run. Soaking even colorfast items for a long period of time may result in color transfer.

Detergent:

Detergent is very important in holding removed soil in suspension and preventing it from redepositing on fabric. Use a generous amount in treating the stain and in laundering the stained garment.

Bleach:

1. Chlorine—Identify by the word *hypochlorite*. This type of bleach may be used on all fabrics except silk, wool, spandex, non-color-fast fabrics, and certain flame-retardant finishes. Follow manufacturer's directions.

2. Oxygen—Identify by words *perborate* or *all-fabric*. This type of bleach may be used on all fabrics and colors. To achieve maximum effectiveness use in warm or hot water with an extended soak or wash time.

Pretreating:

Some stains, especially greasy or oily stains, require pretreating with a solvent before further treatment. Use either a liquid or spray prewash product or a safe spot remover containing perchloroethylene or trichloroethane. These solvents are sold under various brand names. Check labels for ingredients. Use solvents carefully and follow manufacturer's directions. When using these products, add a little extra detergent when laundering the stained item.

CAUTION: Any material on which you have used a cleaning solvent, or which is saturated with flammable liquids or solids, should not be placed in a washer or dryer until all traces of these flammable liquids or solids and their fumes have been removed. There are many highly flammable items used in stain removal procedures, such as acetone, denatured alcohol, some liquid household cleaners, and some spot removers. In addition, stains may be caused by flammable substances, such as turpentine, wax, wax removers, and the like.

Removing an Unknown Stain

When the nature of a stain is not known, follow the sequence of steps described below until the stain is removed.

Since some stains are not easily seen when the fabric is wet, air-dry when indicated to determine whether or not the stain has been removed. Do not machine-dry—for if the stain has not yet been removed, the heat-drying process could make the remaining stain difficult or impossible to remove.

Allow the full time indicated for each step, to give the stain removing agent time to act.

Step One

(a) Soak the stain in cold water for 20 minutes. (b) Work pre-dissolved granular or liquid laundry detergent into stained area, allow to stand for 30 minutes, rinse stained area. (c) Launder in the washer, using the regular cycle, 6–8 minutes of wash time, hot wash, using chlorine bleach for white cottons, nylons, acrylics, polyesters, or rayons; use an oxygen bleach on all other fabrics. Silk or wool articles should be soaked in warm water and agitated very briefly if at all. (d) Air-dry.

Step Two

(a) Soak the stained article overnight using an enzyme presoak according to package directions. (b) Launder in the washer using the regular cycle, 3–5 minutes of wash time. Select hot wash. (c) Air-dry.

Step Three

(a) Sponge stained area thoroughly with trichloroethane. Let stand for 20 minutes. Rub spot with predissolved granular or liquid laundry detergent. Rinse stained area thoroughly. (b) Air-dry.

Step Four

(a) Launder in the washer on the regular cycle, 10 minutes of wash time. Use hot wash water to which RoVer Rust Remover has been added according to the manufacturers' instructions. (b) Air-dry.

Step Five

(a) If the stained fabric can be bleached, mix equal parts of liquid chlorine bleach and water and apply with an eye dropper to stain. Large stained areas can be dipped in the solution. Do not use liquid chlorine bleach on wool, silk, spandex or non-colorfast items— on these fabrics sprinkle oxygen bleach on the stain and dip briefly in very hot or boiling water. (b) Launder immediately in the washer on the regular cycle, 3–5 minutes wash time, hot wash. (c) Air-dry.

If the stain remains after completing all five steps, nothing further can be done to remove it.

Check Color by This Method

Mix 1 tablespoon of bleach with ¼ cup water. Apply one drop of this solution to an inconspicuous portion of the item such as an inside seam. Make sure the solution penetrates the fabric and let stand for one minute. Then blot dry with a paper towel. If there is no color change, then the article can be safely bleached.

Stain Removal Guide

Stain	Removal Procedure for Bleachable Fabrics (white and colorfast cotton, linen, polyester, acrylic, triacetate, nylon, rayon, permanent press)	Removal Procedure for Nonbleachable Fabrics (wool, silk, Spandex, non-colorfast items, some flame retardant finishes—check labels)
Alcoholic beverages	Sponge stain promptly with cold water or soak in cold water for 30 minutes or longer. Rub detergent into any remaining stain while still wet. Launder in hot water using chlorine bleach.	Sponge stain promptly with cold water or soak in cold water for 30 minutes or longer. Sponge with vinegar. Rinse. If stain remains, rub detergent into stain. Rinse. Launder.
Blood	Soak in cold water 30 minutes or longer. Rub detergent into any remaining stain. Rinse. If stain persists, put a few drops of ammonia on the stain and repeat detergent treatment. Rinse. If stain still persists, launder in hot water using chlorine bleach.	Same method, but if colorfastness is questionable, use hydrogen peroxide instead of ammonia. Launder in warm water. Omit chlorine bleach.
Candle wax	Rub with ice cube and carefully scrape off excess wax with a dull knife. Place between several layers of facial tissue or paper towels and press with a warm iron. To remove remaining stain, sponge with safe cleaning fluid. If colored stain remains, launder in hot water using chlorine bleach. Launder again if necessary.	Same method. Launder in warm water. Omit chlorine bleach.
Carbon paper	Rub detergent into dampened stain; rinse well. If stain is not removed, put a few drops of ammonia on the stain and repeat treatment with detergent; rinse well. Repeat if necessary.	Same method, but if colorfastness is questionable, use hydrogen peroxide* instead of ammonia.

Stain	Removal Procedure for Bleachable Fabrics	Removal Procedure for Nonbleachable Fabrics
	(white and colorfast cotton, linen, polyester, acrylic, triacetate, nylon, rayon, permanent press)	(wool, silk, Spandex, non-colorfast items, some flame retardant finishes—check labels)
Catsup	Scrape off excess with a dull knife. Soak in cold water 30 minutes. Rub detergent into stain while still wet and launder in hot water using chlorine bleach.	Same method. Launder in warm water. Omit chlorine bleach.
Chewing gum, adhesive tape	Rub stained area with ice. Remove excess gummy matter carefully with a dull knife. Sponge with a safe cleaning fluid. Rinse and launder.	Same method.
Chocolate and cocoa	Soak in cold water. Rub detergent into stain while still wet, then rinse thoroughly. Dry. If a greasy stain remains, sponge with a safe cleaning fluid. Rinse. Launder in hot water using chlorine bleach. If stain remains, repeat treatment with cleaning fluid.	Same method. Launder in warm water. Omit chlorine bleach.
Coffee, tea	Soak in cold water. Rub detergent into stain while still wet. Rinse and dry. If grease stain remains from cream, sponge with safe cleaning fluid. Launder in hot water using chlorine bleach.	Same method. Launder in warm water. Omit chlorine bleach.
Cosmetics (Eye shadow, lipstick, liquid makeup, mascara, powder, rouge)	Rub detergent into dampened stain until outline of stain is gone, then rinse well. Launder in hot water using chlorine bleach.	Same method. Launder in warm water. Omit chlorine bleach.

Stain	Removal Procedure for Bleachable Fabrics	Removal Procedure for Nonbleachable Fabrics
	(white and colorfast cotton, linen, polyester, acrylic, triacetate, nylon, rayon, permanent press)	(wool, silk, Spandex, non-colorfast items, some flame retardant finishes—check labels)
Crayon	Rub soap (Instant Fels, Ivory Snow, Lux Flakes) into dampened stain, working until outline of stain is removed. Launder in hot water using chlorine bleach. Repeat process if necessary. For stains throughout load of clothes, wash items in hot water using laundry *soap* and 1 cup baking soda. If colored stain remains, launder with a detergent and chlorine bleach.	Same method. Launder in warm water using plenty of detergent. Omit chlorine bleach. If colored stain remains, soak in an enzyme presoak or an oxygen bleach using hottest water safe for fabric; then launder.
Deodorants and antiperspirants	Rub detergent into dampened stain. Launder in hot water using chlorine bleach. Antiperspirants that contain such substances as aluminum chloride are acidic and may change the color of some dyes. Color may or may not be restored by sponging with ammonia. Rinse thoroughly.	Rub detergent into dampened stain. Launder in warm water. Antiperspirants that contain such substances as aluminum chloride are acidic and may change the color of some dyes. Color may or may not be restored by sponging with ammonia. (If ammonia treatment is required, dilute with an equal amount of water for use on wool, mohair, or silk.) Rinse thoroughly.
Dye (transferred from a non-colorfast article)	May be impossible to remove. Bleach immediately using chlorine bleach. Repeat as often as necessary. Or use a commercial color remover.	Use a commercial color remover.

Stain	Removal Procedure for Bleachable Fabrics	Removal Procedure for Nonbleachable Fabrics
	(white and colorfast cotton, linen, polyester, acrylic, triacetate, nylon, rayon, permanent press)	(wool, silk, Spandex, non-colorfast items, some flame retardant finishes—check labels)
Egg, meat juice, and gravy	If dried, scrape off as much as possible with a dull knife. Soak in cold water. Rub detergent into stain while still wet. Launder in hot water using chlorine bleach.	Same method. Launder in warm water. Omit chlorine bleach.
Fabric softener	Rub the dampened stain with bar soap (such as Ivory or Lux) and relaunder in the usual manner.	Same method.
Fingernail polish	Sponge white cotton fabric with nail polish remover; other fabrics with amyl acetate* (banana oil). Launder. Repeat if necessary.	Same method.
Formula	Soak in cold water, then launder in hot water using chlorine bleach. If stain persists, soak in an enzyme presoak.	Soak in warm water using an enzyme presoak. Launder in warm water using plenty of detergent.
Fruit juices	Soak in cold water. Launder in hot water using chlorine bleach.	Soak in cold water. If stain remains, rub detergent into stain while still wet. Launder in warm water.
Grass	Rub detergent into dampened stain. Launder in hot water using chlorine bleach. If stain remains, sponge with alcohol. Rinse thoroughly.	Same method. Launder in warm water. Omit chlorine bleach. If colorfastness is questionable or fabric is acetate, dilute alcohol with two parts water.

Stain	Removal Procedure for Bleachable Fabrics	Removal Procedure for Nonbleachable Fabrics
	(white and colorfast cotton, linen, polyester, acrylic, triacetate, nylon, rayon, permanent press)	(wool, silk, Spandex, non-colorfast items, some flame retardant finishes—check labels)
Grease and oil (car grease, butter, shortening, oily medicines such as oily vitamins)	Rub detergent into dampened stain. Launder in hot water using chlorine bleach and plenty of detergent. If stain persists, sponge thoroughly with safe cleaning fluid. Rinse.	Rub detergent into dampened stain. Launder in warm water using plenty of detergent. If stain persists, sponge thoroughly with safe cleaning fluid. Rinse.
Ink (ballpoint)	Sponge stain with rubbing alcohol, or spray with hair spray until wet looking. Rub detergent into stained area. Launder. Repeat if necessary.	Same method.
Ink, drawing	May be impossible to remove. Run cold water through stain until no more color is being removed. Rub detergent into stain, rinse. Repeat if necessary. Soak in warm sudsy water containing one to four tablespoons of ammonia to a quart of water. Rinse thoroughly. Launder in hot water using chlorine bleach.	Same method. Launder in warm water. Omit chlorine bleach.
Ink from felt tip pen	Rub household cleaner such as 409 or Mr. Clean into stain. Rinse. Repeat as many times as necessary to remove stain. Launder. Some may be impossible to remove.	Same method.
Iodine	Make a solution of sodium thiosulfate crystals.* Use solution to sponge stain. Rinse and launder.	Same method.

Stain	Removal Procedure for Bleachable Fabrics	Removal Procedure for Nonbleachable Fabrics
	(white and colorfast cotton, linen, polyester, acrylic, triacetate, nylon, rayon, permanent press)	(wool, silk, Spandex, non-colorfast items, some flame retardant finishes—check labels)
Mayonnaise, salad dressing	Rub detergent into dampened stain. Rinse and let dry. If greasy stain remains, sponge with safe cleaning fluid. Rinse. Launder in hot water with chlorine bleach.	Same method. Launder in warm water. Omit chlorine bleach.
Mildew	Rub detergent into dampened stain. Launder in hot water using chlorine bleach. If stain remains, sponge with hydrogen peroxide.* Rinse and launder.	Same method. Launder in warm water. Omit chlorine bleach.
Milk, cream, ice cream	Soak in cold water. Launder in hot water using chlorine bleach. If grease stain remains, sponge with safe cleaning fluid. Rinse.	Soak in cold water. Rub detergent into stain. Launder. If grease stain remains, sponge with safe cleaning fluid. Rinse.
Mustard	Rub detergent into dampened stain. Rinse. Soak in hot detergent water for several hours. If stain remains, launder in hot water using chlorine bleach.	Same method. Launder in warm water. Omit chlorine bleach.
Paint and varnish	Treat stains quickly before paint dries. If a solvent is recommended as a thinner, sponge it onto stain. Turpentine or trichloroethane can be used. While stain is still wet with solvent, work detergent into stain and soak in hot water. Then launder. Repeat procedure if stain remains after laundering. Stain may be impossible to remove.	Same method.

Stain	Removal Procedure for Bleachable Fabrics	Removal Procedure for Nonbleachable Fabrics
	(white and colorfast cotton, linen, polyester, acrylic, triacetate, nylon, rayon, permanent press)	(wool, silk, Spandex, non-colorfast items, some flame retardant finishes—check labels)
Perfume	Same as alcoholic beverages.	Same as alcoholic beverages.
Perspiration	Rub detergent into dampened stain. Launder in hot water using chlorine bleach. If fabric has discolored, try to restore it by treating fresh stains with ammonia or old stains with vinegar. Rinse. Launder.	Same method. Launder in warm water. Omit chlorine bleach.
Ring around the collar	Apply liquid laundry detergent or a paste of granular detergent and water on the stain. Let it set for 30 minutes. A prewash product especially designed for this purpose may be used. Follow manufacturer's directions. Launder.	Same method.
Rust	Launder in hot water with detergent and RoVer® Rust Remover. Follow manufacturer's instructions. RoVer is available from authorized Maytag dealers and parts distributors; specify Part No. 57961.	Same method. If colorfastness is questionable, test a concealed area first.
Scorch	Launder in hot water using chlorine bleach or RoVer Rust Remover, (see Rust). Severe scorching cannot be removed; fabric has been damaged.	Cover stains with cloth dampened with hydrogen peroxide. Cover with a dry cloth and press with an iron as hot as is safe for fabric. Rinse thoroughly. Rub detergent into stained area while still wet. Launder. Repeat if necessary.

Stain	Removal Procedure for Bleachable Fabrics	Removal Procedure for Nonbleachable Fabrics
	(white and colorfast cotton, linen, polyester, acrylic, triacetate, nylon, rayon, permanent press)	(wool, silk, Spandex, non-colorfast items, some flame retardant finishes—check labels)
Shoe polish (wax)	Scrape off as much as possible with a dull knife. Rub detergent into dampened stain. Launder in hot water using chlorine bleach. If stain persists, sponge with rubbing alcohol. Rinse. Launder.	Scrape off as much as possible with a dull knife. Rub detergent into dampened stain. Launder in warm water. If stain persists, sponge with one part alcohol and two parts water. Rinse. Launder.
Soft drinks	Sponge stain immediately with cold water. Launder in hot water with chlorine bleach. Some drink stains are invisible after they dry, but turn yellow with aging or heating. This yellow stain may be impossible to remove.	Same method. Launder in warm water. Omit chlorine bleach.
Tar and asphalt	Act quickly before stain is dry. Pour trichloroethane through cloth. Repeat. Stain may be impossible to remove. Rinse and launder.	Same method.
Urine	Soak in cold water. Rub detergent into stain. Launder in hot water using chlorine bleach. If the color of the fabric has been altered by stain, sponge with ammonia; rinse thoroughly. If stain persists, sponging with vinegar may help.	Same method. Launder in warm water. Omit chlorine bleach. If ammonia treatment is necessary, dilute ammonia with an equal part of water for use on wool, mohair, or silk.
Wine	Same treatment as for alcoholic beverages. Wait 15 minutes and rinse. Repeat if necessary.	Same treatment as for alcoholic beverages.

Stain	Removal Procedure for Bleachable Fabrics	Removal Procedure for Nonbleachable Fabrics
	(white and colorfast cotton, linen, polyester, acrylic, triacetate, nylon, rayon, permanent press)	(wool, silk, Spandex, non-colorfast items, some flame retardant finishes—check labels)
Yellowing of white cottons and linens	Fill washer with very hot water. Add at least twice as much detergent as normal. Place articles in washer and agitate for four minutes on regular cycle. Stop washer and add one cup of chlorine bleach to the bleach dispenser or dilute in one quart of water and pour around agitator. Restart washer at once. Agitate four minutes. Stop washer and allow articles to soak 15 minutes. Restart washer and set ten minute wash time; allow washer to complete normal cycle. Repeat entire procedure two or more consecutive times until whiteness is restored.	
Yellowing of white nylon	Soak 15 to 30 minutes in solution of ⅛ cup of chlorine bleach and one teaspoon of vinegar thoroughly mixed with each gallon of warm water. Rinse. Repeat if necessary.	

Note: This chart applies only to washable items. It does not apply to garments which should be dry-cleaned. Some stains are not easily seen when the fabric is wet. Air-dry the articles to be certain the stain has been removed. Machine drying might make the stain more difficult to remove. Prewash products may be more convenient to use in treating stains than the process of rubbing detergent into the dampened stain. *Available at drugstore.

TEARS

If a garment gets a rip or hole in it, try to repair it as soon as possible so that it does not get worse. If you are not good with a sewing machine or with a needle and thread, take the item to a seamstress. Once the item has been repaired, have your child try it on. If it no longer looks chic on him or her, you are best off giving the garment away. Patches can sometimes look attractive in a rough, informal way—but on some kids or garments they just look ugly.

CLOSET ORGANIZATION

Part of good wardrobe maintenance is good organization. A well-organized closet is one where everything can easily be seen and reached. Your child should be able to walk into the closet, see what's there, and take out what he or she wants. The closet should be light enough to look around in, and he or she should

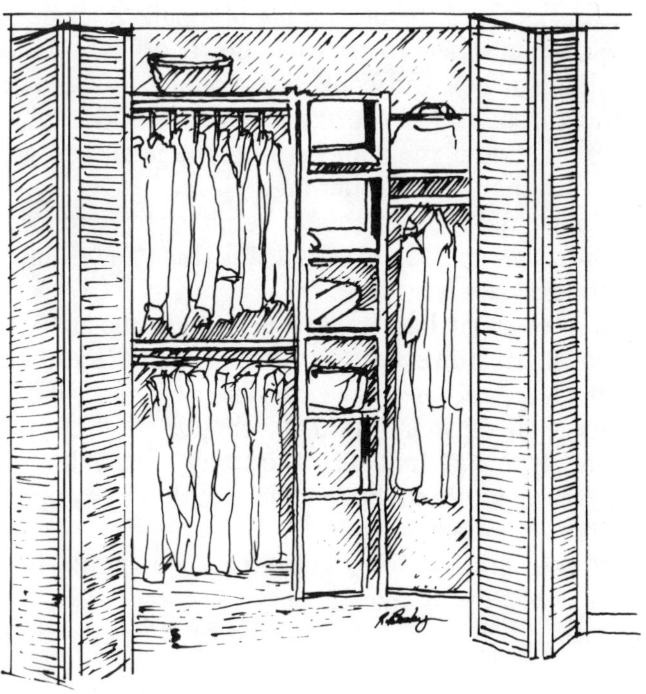

be able to reach everything in it. This probably means lowering the pole, but that's hardly a difficult job, and it will make things much easier for both you and your child. Hooks should be lowered, too, if necessary.

For maximum ease in finding and selecting clothes, put all your child's shirts together in one part of the closet, all the pants in another part, and so on. If items are stored in boxes or drawers, it is helpful to label everything clearly.

SHOE CARE

Shoes and boots require their own special kind of care. The best way to care for a pair of leather shoes is to keep them polished, protect them from moisture, and give them some rest by not wearing the same pair every day. This last bit of shoe care is easy for children, who don't wear leather shoes that often, anyway. However, you should teach your children to polish and care for their own shoes from the time they are seven or eight.

Here are some other tips for children's footwear:

1. Never store or leave footwear near a source of heat. This can take months off the life of a pair of shoes or boots.
2. Children's heels can wear down quickly. Check your child's shoes and boots occasionally to see if any heels need repairing. Putting on a new heel doesn't cost that much, and if you wait too long, the heels can wear down so far that they cannot be replaced.
3. Your child's shoes should be polished regularly. This is the single most important thing that can be done to make shoes last a long time.
4. If your child has suede shoes, these do not need to be polished. However, it is very important that they be kept as clean and as dry as possible between wearings. Buy some suede stain guard at a shoe store. Make sure shoes are clean and dry before the spray is used. If suede shoes get wet, let them dry out thoroughly, then apply an extra coat of protective spray.
5. If your child's shoes get dirty, they should be brushed or wiped off as soon as possible.
6. Athletic shoes can be cleaned by throwing them in the

washer. They should be air-dried, however. Never put them in a hot dryer.

7. Sandpaper used on the soles of new shoes will make them less slippery.
8. To slip new boots on and off more easily, spray the inside with silicone.
9. Leather laces will stay tied better if you sprinkle a few drops of water on the knot.
10. Shoes should be wiped off before polishing. Use a polish that not only soaks in and polishes the leather but also cleans it.
11. For heavily scuffed areas, use an enriched polish with color-coating ability.
12. Apply waxes sparingly, and don't use heavy oils on delicate leathers.
13. If shoes or boots get stained from snow or salt, mix a solution of equal parts of warm water and white vinegar. Gently pat this on the stain and entire shoe. Allow to dry and then polish.

15

Good Grooming

GOOD GROOMING IS A BASIC AND essential part of kids' chic. A dirty or ill-groomed child never looks attractive, no matter how perfect his or her features are and no matter how well he or she is dressed. A well-groomed child, on the other hand, tends to look happier and more attractive no matter what he or she is doing or wearing.

You should teach your children proper grooming habits from the time they are very small. Kids are almost never too young to start taking care of their own appearance. Even a child of two can learn some of the basics of good grooming. And, like many other things, regular grooming habits become easier as they become part of your child's regular routine. Teaching your child proper grooming may be difficult at first, but with patience and persistence, the good habits will slowly sink in.

Here are some tips to make grooming easier for both parents and kids:

CLEANLINESS

Regular bathing is the first step in any grooming routine. Bathing does not have to take a great deal of time or effort—sponge baths or showers work just fine, and they take only five to ten minutes. Soap, a washcloth, a sponge, and a nail brush are all basic equipment. Nail brushes are good for getting out ground-in dirt on feet, knees, hands, and elbows as well as nails.

If you want your child to shampoo his or her hair while taking a shower or bath, make sure the shampoo is in easy reach. Shatter-proof plastic bottles for shampoo and cream rinse are, of course, a must. Squeeze containers are easiest for children to use. Toys can entice kids into the tub. Squirt guns, toy boats, or sculptured soaps in the form of favorite superheroes are inexpensive and fun for the bath.

Some children may have an adverse skin reaction to some soaps or bubble baths. If this is the case, use a neutral or balanced pH soap. These soaps, which come in both solid and liquid form, work just as well and will not cause rashes or allergic reactions. Phisoderm and Neutrogena are examples. A wide range of products are available for coloring the bathwater and softening children's skin, but many of these are actually harsh on children's skin, especially in the winter. Children get along better with thinner washcloths rather than thicker facecloths that are difficult for little hands to use.

While soap removes dirt, perspiration, and body oil, most of it is detergent based and can dry out your child's skin. Therefore, make sure that your youngster rinses soap and shampoo *thoroughly* from his or her body and hair at the end of a bath or shower. If your child has dry skin, shorter baths or showers and

warm rather than hot water will be better. Thorough drying helps to remove dead skin and stimulates circulation. Kids seem to love wrapping themselves up in big, plush, colorful towels, so you may want to have some on hand.

After your child bathes in the wintertime, you may want to use a moisturizing lotion to soften his or her skin and prevent chapping and chafing. In the summer, baby powder and corn starch help children to stay cooler and dryer.

Around the age of ten, many boys and girls may begin to use deodorants or antiperspirants. Although there are no specific children's deodorants on the market, some products are definitely milder than others. You may need to experiment to find the right one for your child, so buy small sizes at first. Perfume in deodorants can cause irritation; unscented deodorants and antiperspirants are more appropriate for children.

SKIN

Sometimes it's all a parent can do to get kids to wash their face and hands with soap. It's a good idea to teach your child to rinse his or her hands and face thoroughly after washing them and to use clean washcloths, since soap drying on his or her face or hands can irritate the skin. Or, if your child prefers, allow him or her to suds the hands into a lather rather than use a washcloth.

Make sure your children wash their entire faces rather than just their cheeks (cheeks-only is a common practice among kids). Teach your child to wash across the forehead and down the center of the face, especially on the sides of his or her nose. These are areas in which oiliness is most likely to occur.

Complexion problems can appear in children at any age, but they are most common with the onset of the hormonal changes that occur during puberty. Acne, blemishes, whiteheads, and blackheads are not just due to dirty hands and faces. Acne is caused by clogged pores and the excessive oils that the body produces during adolescence. While there is no one cure for acne, there are means to assist in preventing and clearing it. Nevertheless, cleanliness is still the best weapon against blemishes.

If your child develops chapped skin, there are several ointments available over the counter that provide excellent relief, even for heavily chapped areas.

TEETH

Of course, brushing twice a day is one of the first habits you'll try to teach. It is important that the head of your child's toothbrush is small enough to reach all the surfaces of each of his or her teeth; yet the toothbrush should still be easy to handle. Soft brushes are the ones most recommended by dentists. You may need to assist a young child in brushing his or her teeth. Once your children have learned to brush by themselves, you should still check periodically to make sure they are brushing properly and getting at every surface of every tooth. The tendency to rush through tooth brushing and miss a tooth or two is common to everyone—adults included.

Daily use of dental floss is also considered a basic part of proper hygiene. You may need to floss very young children's teeth yourself. Also, you should supervise children who are fairly new at flossing for themselves. It is difficult to reach the back teeth, and proper flossing is no easy task for children. But it gets much easier with practice.

NAILS

Little fingers, especially those that make mud pies, get a lot of dirt embedded under the nails, in the cuticles, and all around the hands. Besides a nail brush, an emery board or nail file, an orange stick, and a nail clipper are all necessary pieces of equipment. Clippers work better than manicure scissors, and they are easier and much less dangerous for children to use.

Toenails should be cut straight across to prevent ingrown toenails, but fingernails should be cut in a rounded shape. Be careful not to cut down too close to the cuticles. An emery board or polishing circle works well for smoothing nail surfaces. Also, a dead skin or callus remover such as Pretty Feet or Dr. Scholl's Dead Skin Remover will remove hangnails or rough dead skin around the nails.

An orange stick is handy to use to push back the cuticle. This should only be done after a bath, after soaking the nails in warm water, or after softening the nail area with a lotion or cream. Vaseline Intensive Care lotion, A&D Ointment, or Arden's 8-Hour Cream are excellent to rub into cuticles for deep moisturizing.

A common problem with kids is nail biting. It is partly caused by very dry and itchy skin in the cuticle area—the biting is a form of scratching. If the area is moisturized and cared for regularly, there is less of an urge to bite. Once the nail biting becomes a habit, however, it is difficult to break even when there is no more itching, so try to relieve the itching early on.

HAIR

The health of the hair is affected by almost everything in your child's life, including diet, sunlight, air pollution, medication, stress, blow drying, general health, permanents, shampoos, conditioners, and so on. The number of hair follicles you are born with remains constant throughout your life. Hair coarseness or fineness is also a hereditary trait that does not normally change. It is also impossible to do anything to make a baby's hair grow until it is ready to do so. Each child's rate of hair growth is as individual as his or her rate of learning to speak or walk. By the time a child reaches three to four years of age, though, you will know what kind of hair he or she will have. While the color may change with age, you will know whether your child's hair will be thick or thin, fine or coarse.

In general, you should treat young children's hair gently, washing it regularly and avoiding hard brushing. When you pick a shampoo or conditioner for your child's hair, you should use the same good judgment and care that you do when you choose your own. Baby shampoos were developed so that they would not sting children's eyes during shampooing. However, most baby shampoos are very harsh chemically and are not considered to be good for the hair because of their poor pH balance. Conditioners make children's hair easier to handle and less prone to snarls and breakage. Conditioners and finishing rinses are especially helpful for children with fine hair or long hair and for those who live in sunny climates. Basically, the kind of shampoo and conditioner you select for your child should feel good on your hands—this can tell you a lot and is a reliable test.

Your child should always use as little shampoo and conditioner as possible to get the job done, but he or she should use both. Children have a tendency to rinse their hair too little, so make sure they rinse, rinse, rinse. Then they should rinse some more.

Training children about proper hair care can be a trying experience. Many young kids cry and make a fuss; some can't stand having another person wash their hair. It can be a real battleground. But, if you can make hair washing a treat instead of a chore or a punishment, most children can learn to love it.

One good way to teach your young children to wash their own hair is to take a shower with them. Wash your hair in the shower, and have your child mimic you. Encourage heavy rinsing by allowing your child to play and splash. The accent should always be on fun!

After getting out of the water, first dry your child's hair by patting it with a towel. All hair is weakest when wet, and rubbing can tangle and damage it. Next, a very wide-tooth comb is useful for removing tangles. (Never use a narrow-toothed comb—it can get snagged very easily and cause pain.) You should always comb the ends of your child's hair out first, and teach him or her to do the same. This is healthier and more comfortable than dragging or snagging a comb all the way through it. After this you can blow-dry or naturally air-dry your child's hair very easily.

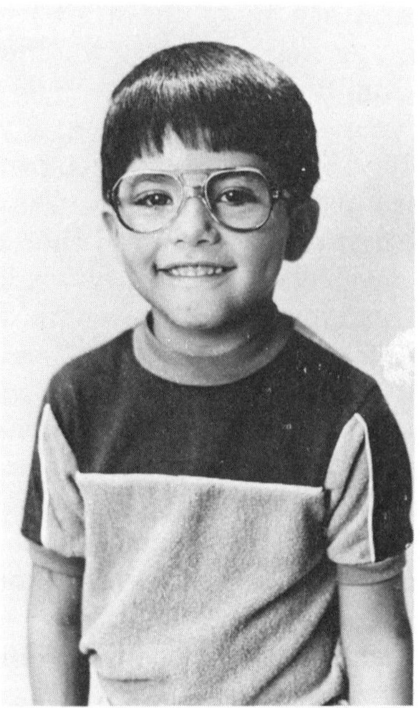

On kids, hair styles that follow the way the hair falls naturally look best and are the easiest to care for.

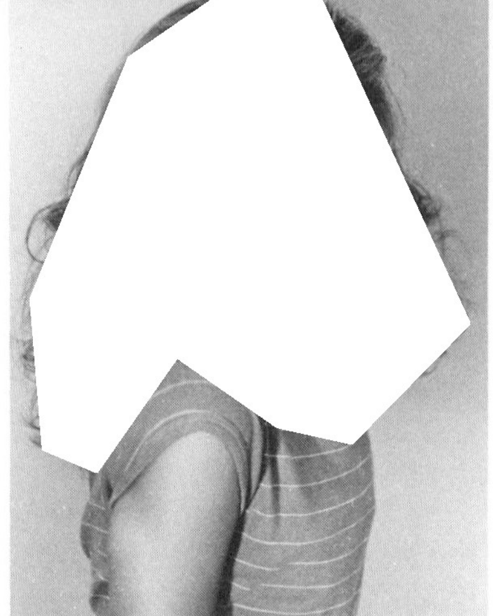

As a general rule, children's hair should be cut, styled, and treated as naturally as possible. Children's hair is more fragile than adults', so little girls who wear tight pigtails or ponytails can damage their hair and cause hair loss if their hair is pulled constantly and tightly. Covered rubber bands, loose braids, and occasionally changing your child's part will all help alleviate this regular pulling. Permanents and hair-straightening lotions break the hair more easily in children than in adults, so caution is best.

Diet affects the hair of children as well as that of adults. Eating too much fat or sugar is harmful to the hair. Encourage children to drink plenty of water each day and to eat fresh fruits and vegetables. Children who have beautiful, shiny, healthy-looking hair almost always have well-balanced diets.

16

Teaching Your Child to Make His or Her Own Chic

Y OU NOW KNOW NEARLY EVERY-thing we do about helping your child look and feel as attractive as possible. Now you are ready for the final part of kids' chic: passing it on to your child.

If you can start teaching your child about clothing and grooming at a young age, the principles of kids' chic will sink in more and more each year, and by the time your child is a teenager, his or her own particular brand of chic will come naturally.

Below are some hints for teaching children of different ages about kids' chic:

AGES ONE THROUGH SIX

- Look at some pictures of children in current magazines and catalogs together. Ask your child to express her or his preference in colors, fabrics, designs, and styles.
- When you do a color test on your child, explain why you are doing it and how it works.
- While you are shopping, explain to your child why a certain color or design looks good on her or him—or why a certain style or color doesn't.

- Explain what making a clothing purchase is. Show your child price tags and explain prices. Show her or him money, checks, and charge cards; let your child hold them and look at them up close. Explain how each of these works.
- Show your child the tags on clothing. Explain how garments come in different sizes, and tell your child her or his sizes.
- In the morning, give your child some choice of what she or he will wear that day.
- Begin teaching proper grooming habits.

AGES SEVEN THROUGH TEN

- Show your child all of his or her measurements; have your son or daughter watch as you take them. Show your child his or her sizes in the charts in Chapter 7.
- Encourage your child to choose his or her own outfits. Critique his or her selections; if the clothes your child has chosen go well together, say so and explain why. If they do not, explain why they do not.
- When you go shopping, show your child how and why some designs look good on him or her and why some do not.
- Ask your child to show you some items he or she likes in the store.
- Explain to your child about a few of the basic fibers and their characteristics. Wool, cotton, and polyester are probably enough.
- Look through clothing ads and catalogs with your child, showing him or her a wide variety of styles and designs. Ask your son or daughter to point out items he or she likes.
- Put together a clothing scrapbook with your child. This should be a book of items he or she would like to wear. If possible, it should cover many different styles and occasions and clothing for all four seasons.
- Teach your child to spot three- and four-season clothing.
- As much as possible, make all decisions on clothing purchases jointly with your child.

- Explain the principles of color combining to your child. Have him or her make up some sample outfits based on these principles.
- If your child would like a new basic color, you and he or she should pick one together.
- Teach your child to care for and polish his or her own shoes.
- Teach your child the M & M Point System (Chapter 6).

AGES ELEVEN THROUGH THIRTEEN

- Explain wardrobe planning to your children. Let them have some practice planning out additions to their wardrobe. Critique the selections.
- Teach your children to wash, dry, and put away their own clothes. Show them the labels on clothing, and explain the importance of following the directions exactly.
- Let your children make some of their own clothing selections and purchases while you watch. Comment on their selections.
- Teach your children about line and design (Chapter 4).
- Explain to your children how to spot quality in clothing (Chapter 9).
- Help your children shop for accessories, and show them how to make appropriate selections (Chapter 6).
- Teach your children about the four key points of kids' chic (Chapter 3).
- Teach your children to use the Clothing Efficiency Formula (Chapter 11).
- Explain to your children about versatility in clothing.

Part VI

Who's Making Kids' Clothing Today

17

Designers and Manufacturers with Style

To MAKE OUTFITTING YOUR child easier, you should know some specifics about the various designers and manufacturers. These firms vary widely, not only in their styles but also in the kinds of clothing they make, the markets they want to target, and their basic philosophies about children's clothing. Some, for example, believe that children should look like children, not like little adults. As a result, their clothes will have an unmistakeable little-girl or little-boy look—charming and innocent. Others see absolutely nothing wrong with adapting the latest adult or teen fashions to a kids' line: that's what they set out to do. Esprit is an example of a company that made its first spash with up-to-date teen fashions and then carried the look over into a children's line. Often a kids' line originates when the maker of a popular kind of adult clothing senses a demand for the same thing in kids' sizes. Oshkosh B'Gosh, Ocean Pacific and Merona Sport Childrenswear began in this way. In such cases, it's clear that the adult and children's lines will have the same recognizable look.

In this chapter, we describe fourteen prominent children's clothing makers: the kinds of items they make, their strong points, their signature looks. Although there's a good chance that these names are familiar to you, the ones we have included are not necessarily the biggest or the most important. (There are hundreds of makers of kids' clothing, and we don't have the space to discuss all of the important ones here.) Our intent is to give you some good consumer information, as well as a sense of the variety of approaches that different companies take to the same basic task of creating clothes for kids.

ABSORBA

For high-quality, pure cotton clothing, especially in infants' and toddlers' sizes, Absorba is a name that has enjoyed increasing popularity in recent years. The American division of this 175-year-old French company offers layette clothing for infants, infants' and toddlers' sportswear, and cotton sportswear—turtlenecks, sweaters, overalls, and T-shirts—for older children. Quality is high, and items tend to be priced upscale. Absorba's look is simple and sophisticated; clothes are cut narrow and are closely fitted, as opposed to the more boxy American look. These factors, plus the choice of colors and prints, give Absorba clothes a distinctive European feeling.

Boys' and girls' sizes start with layette and newborn and go up to size 14.

> Absorba, Inc.
> 112 West 34 St.
> New York, New York 10120
> (212) 947–6024

CEIL AINSWORTH

Ceil Ainsworth is best known for bringing back the pinafore. "When my daughter Susan was a baby," says Ceil Ainsworth, "I wanted to dress her in pinafores like the ones I wore when I was a little girl, but I couldn't find them anywhere. So I decided to make Susan one myself."

Other parents who want the same Alice in Wonderland look for their very young girls can find Ceil Ainsworth creations in children's specialty stores and better department stores. A wide variety of pinafore aprons layered over dresses is available in the smaller sizes. In sizes for older girls, the line tends toward sophisticated and versatile "go anywhere" dresses. Shirt dresses are a favored style for preteens. The company designs very little sportswear.

Most aprons are made of delicate white fabrics; some pinafore-dress outfits will combine prints—wallpaper stripes and calico, for example. Ceil Ainsworth makes a point of choosing fabrics that are easy to wash and easy to care for.

Sizes range from infant to preteen.

> Ceil Ainsworth
> 131 West 33 St.
> New York, New York 10001
> (212) 695–9227

BULL FROG KNITS

If the jogging suit has become a staple of your child's wardrobe, then you may already know about Bull Frog Knits. Their fleece warm-up suits, often jazzed up with satin appliqués or details in contrasting fabrics, are available in better department stores. Boys' and girls' fine knit sets and activewear complete the line. Garments are comfortable, durable, colorfast, and easy to launder.

Beach scenes and themes predominate in the recently opened Panama Jack division of Bull Frog. Screen-printed outdoor scenes, animals, art deco images, and camouflage patterns decorate the fleece garments in this line.

Sizes for the boys' and girls' knit sets start at newborn and go up to 6X. Sizes for fleece jogging suits and activewear range from newborn through preteen for girls and size 18 for boys. Prices for knit sets range from $20.00 to $33.00, and prices for fleece jogging suits range from $20.00 to $37.00.

> Bull Frog Knits
> 112 West 34 St.
> New York, New York 10120
> (212) 695–2282

CALABASH AND DOESPUN

Calabash, which produces trendy sportswear and denims, is a popular brand of moderately priced clothing for boys and girls.

Doespun, its parent company, is strong in the infant-to-toddler age group. Garments are made from blended fabrics. One specialty store owner we talked with likes the comfort and price of Doespun's cotton/poly knit sets and often recommends them to parents who ask. Calabash and Doespun clothes are available from better retailers and specialty stores across the country.

> Calabash
> Doespun
> 131 West 33 St.
> New York, New York 10001
> (212) 279–6844

FLORENCE EISEMAN

Parents associate Florence Eiseman's name with dressy, classic dresses in elegant fabrics. Other distinguishing ingredients in the Florence Eiseman look are clear, cheerful colors, fine tailoring, lots of appliqués in all sizes, and for those unenchanted with appliqués, sophisticated sewn-in details on other items, such as piping around collars and sleeves, pleated sleeves, and quilted belts. Garments are kept simple, allowing the natural charm of the child to predominate.

For the spring season, there are four collections: the designer collection (dresses), knit separates, swimwear, and infants' clothing (all pastels). In the fall, the swimwear line is replaced by sweaters, and a small holiday collection of very dressy clothes is brought out late in the season. Tyrolean outfits for brothers and sisters and one or two brother/sister tartan plaid outfits are favorites in the yearly fall line.

According to one store owner, mothers who come in often make a special request for Florence Eiseman dresses. Her clothes have a reputation for outlasting several hand-me-down users.

Girls' sizes start at 0 for infants and go up to size 14. Boys' sizes range from 0 to 7. Prices range from $16.00 to $110.00, with most styles priced at $40.00.

> Florence Eiseman
> 301 North Water St.
> Milwaukee, Wisconsin 53202
> (414) 272–3222

ESPRIT

Matching the success of its stylish sportswear for teens, Esprit more recently made a splash with its children's collection. Esprit's look is sporty and sophisticated with clean lines and bright colors—no fuss. Bold stripes and gingham plaids or white and geometric designs on sweaters and sweat shirts are common. The summer collection includes coordinated shorts and tops, jump suits, cotton pants, tank tops and T-shirts, jumpers, skirts, and sundresses. Prices are generally moderate.

> Esprit/Kids
> Esprit de Corp
> 900 Minnesota St.
> San Francisco, California 94107
> (415) 648–6900

POLLY FLINDERS

Hand-smocked dresses are this company's special trademark. Smocking on dresses, shirts, and blouses is an art that can be traced back to thirteenth-century England. But by the nineteenth century, English workers had adopted the smock, using specific designs to identify their trade or occupation. Polly Flinders selects from a vast library of delicate designs; trained craftsworkers in the Caribbean islands of Barbados and St. Vincent then hand-stitch the dresses. Each dress takes about three hours of work to complete.

Sizes range from newborn to size 14. Prices are between $14.00 and $34.00: the average price for a dress is $26.00.

> Polly Flinders
> The Baylis Brothers Company
> 224 East 5th St.
> Cincinnati, Ohio 45202
> (513)721–7020

NORMA KAMALI

In describing children of the 1980s and Norma Kamali's clothing designs, one discovers a common ground: movement,

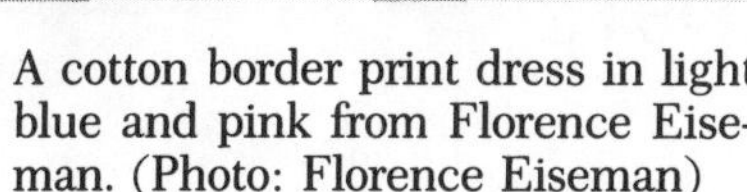

A cotton border print dress in light blue and pink from Florence Eiseman. (Photo: Florence Eiseman)

Polly Flinders combines ruffles, bows and plaids in this dress for very young girls. (Photo: Polly Flinders)

energy, and creativity. Her great ideas seem as well suited to the contemporary child as they have been to the modern woman. Shapes are versatile; clothes are wearable, washable and easy to combine. Norma Kamali's Kids Fashions are on the cover of this book. Kamali's name is synonomous with fashionable sweatshirt dressing in girls' sizes 2 to 4, toddler, 4 to 6X, and 7 to 14. She also offers a variety of outfits in pure cotton flannel. Kamali's clothes are easy-care garments. (Shoulder pads are attached with velcro for immediate removal when laundering.) They are sized with practical fullness for freedom of movement and longevity of wear. Prices are affordable.

Norma Kamali's Kid's Fashions are available in major department stores nationwide.

Norma Kamali's Kids
A Division of Empire Shield Company, Inc.
112 West 34 St.
New York, New York 10120
(212) 736–2330

CALVIN KLEIN

Calvin Klein understands the American lifestyle—he knows how we live and work. He strongly believes in the concept of total dressing and designs seasonless quality garments using natural fabrics and classic colorations. His simply yet sophisticated style carries through in his clothes for boys as well. Calvin Klein boyswear collection includes activewear dresswear, outerwear, and accessories. All colorations and fabrications are designed to work well with one another. Fleece shirts go well with denim pants; woven shirts blend with casual or dressy trousers.

> Calvin Klein Jeans
> Division of Puritan Fashions
> 1400 Broadway
> New York, New York 10018
> (212) 575–0800

IZOD LACOSTE

Besides the famous Lacoste knit shirt, Izod makes fancy knit shirts, wool and acrylic sweaters, outerwear, pants, skirts, jumpers, overalls, shorts, infants' stretch sleepers, and swimwear. The largest percentage of the company's business is in boys' clothing, with the girls' and infants' lines running close together in sales.

Blended fabrics predominate, although some sweaters, shirts, pants, and jackets are made of pure cotton. A special plus for parents is Izod's attention to construction details. In the children's line, double-stitched seams make pants more durable. On the knit shirts, inside collar and shoulder seams are stitched with tape, so they don't scratch. Infants' clothes have snap shoulders and crotches, for ease in dressing and undressing. On infants' outerwear and zipper-fronted sweaters, Velcro closings over the top of the zipper help keep the baby warm and guard against catching the baby's skin in the zipper.

For girls, sizes range from newborn to preteen. Boys' clothing runs to size 20.

> Izod for Children
> 11 Penn Plaza
> New York, New York 10018
> (212) 502–3000

RALPH LAUREN

Ralph Lauren has always believed that fashion is a function of lifestyle. He designs clothes that are natural to the way people really live today—that are as easy and nonchalant as a pair of jeans, that mix well, and that don't go out of style tomorrow but instead become more personal and special as they're worn. A purist who uses natural fabrics, he avoids gimmicks and concentrates on developing and perfecting the classics. His boys' clothes are essentially miniaturized versions of his Polo menswear. There are shaped blazers and hacking jackets, tailored shirts in pure cotton, rugged pants and pleated flannels, distinctive sweaters—clothes that are relaxed enough for the schoolyard yet fine enough for a party.

Ralph Lauren Girls' Collection was a natural follow-up to his boy's clothing. His collection for young girls, sizes 7 to 14, is an effortless juxtaposition of lace and tweeds, flannel and velvet. Items range from smocked dresses with lace collars to sturdy tweed hacking jackets and from pinafores to corduroy jeans.

Ralph Lauren
Polo Fashions
40 West 55 St.
New York, New York 10019
(212) 603–2600

Merona Sport creates a sporty but soft look with this bibbed wool jumper and buffalo plaid shirt. (Photo: Merona Sport)

MERONA SPORT

Begun as a menswear company in 1978, Merona Sport based its original collection on the uniforms of a rugby team in New Zealand. The look here is sporty and all-American—as the company's ads make clear—and the bright, easy-to-blend rugby colors are still Merona Sport's trademark. Other virtues that have made their fashions popular are the pure natural fabrics and the construction details: athletic grommets on shirts (vents in the seams), canvas taping to reinforce seams, drawstring waists, and locker loops. Rugby shirts for boys are the bestsellers in this line. New items for kids are bathing suits and outerwear.

Merona Sport
30 Rockefeller Plaza, Suite 3450
New York, New York 10112
(212) 586–7289

OCEAN PACIFIC

Ocean Pacific makes durable coordinated sportswear for adults and kids; the kids' lines adapt the styles of the adults' collection. Items include woven shirts; knit shirts; swim trunks; walk shorts in corduroy, canvas, and twill; pants; jackets; and accessories. The girls' line also includes skirts and pedal pushers. Distinctive features in OP clothes are a generous cut and bright colors. Natural fabrics predominate. The California-livin' theme is strongly evident. The company began as a maker of surfboards and swim trunks, and today beach scenes, palm trees, and Pacific sunsets are still favorite images on the screen-printed T-shirts.

While the company is located in California and does a majority of its business in the West and Southwest, it is quickly catching on in the Northeast and Midwest. Apparently the growing reputation of the OP men's clothing created in its wake an increased consumer demand for the boys' and girls' clothing as well.

Sizes in the boys' lines are 4 to 7 and 8 to 20; girls' sizes are 7 to 14. For the spring of 1985, the company plans to launch a girls' line in 4 to 6X. It does not make clothes for infants and toddlers.

Ocean Pacific
1200 Valencia
Tustin, California 92680
(714) 731–1181

OSHKOSH B'GOSH

Although the company has existed for almost a hundred years, it was only three or four years ago that its childrenswear business really started to take off. Apparently, kids as well as adults enjoy owning the real thing, and when it comes to overalls, Oshkosh is undoubtedly the real thing. Founded in 1895 as a maker of work clothes for farmers, Oshkosh B'Gosh now turns out infant sleepwear, children's knit tops, sweaters, jackets, western-style jeans, caps, tote bags, backpacks, and of course, the classic bib overall. Overalls are made of denim, corduroy, and cotton drill. Stylish adaptations in the girls' line are baggy denim overalls in pastels, stripes, and checks. The down-home chic extends into the infants' line with a new item: denim or corduroy bib overalls with feet. Also worthy of note is their Hotliner program, which offers flannel overalls and pants.

Clothes are available in infants', toddlers', boys', and girls' sizes. Prices range from $15.00 to $25.00 for most items.

Oshkosh B'Gosh
112 East Otter St.
Oshkosh, Wisconsin 54901
(414) 231–8800

PETIT BATEAU

This French-based company makes appealing, high quality playwear and underclothes in classic styles for infants and toddlers, most of which are sold in children's specialty shops. Both the designs and the fabrics come from France, although the clothes are actually produced in the United States. Nearly all garments are 100 percent cotton and can be machine washed with minimum shrinkage. Petit Bateau's soft colors and delicate decoration make these outfits favorite gifts.

> Petit Bateau U.S.A., Inc.
> 104 Friends Lane
> Newtown, Pennsylvania 18940
> (215) 968–9606

POPSICLE

If you would like to see your children in clothes that look charming and playful, as opposed to trendy or sophisticated, then Popsicle is a name that you will want to check out. The firm makes sportswear, school clothes, and play clothes in infants' sizes and boys' and girls' 4 to 6X. (Dreamsicle is a related line for girls in the 7 to 14 size range.) Appliqués abound; puffy appliqués that seem to pop out are a particularly whimsical touch. In the basic sportswear line, special attention is paid to practical details (extra pockets on overalls, for example). Pretty handmade acrylic sweaters, priced at $15.00, are a particularly good buy. In general, clothes are moderately priced.

> Popsicle Playwear
> 112 West 34 St., Room 1507
> New York, New York 10001
> (212) 594–5511

LEVI STRAUSS

Levi Strauss, founded in the 1800s and still family-owned, is the world's largest manufacturer of brand-name clothing. For the record, the company has sold more than 2 billion pairs of jeans. The basic jeans in children's sizes are made of denim, corduroy, and twill fabrics; they feature copper rivets or bar tacking at the stress points and double stitching at the seams. Other offerings in the Youthwear lines are "Koveralls" and "shortalls," woven and knit shirts, slacks and blazers, and a wide variety of other activewear. The company pays special attention to fit, and most clothes from toddlers' sizes on up are available in both regular and slim sizes. The boys' line features husky and students' sizes as well. Prices are moderate.

Levi Strauss
Levi's Plaza
1155 Battery Street
San Francisco, California 94106
(415) 544–6000

A standby for parents: the reliable Levi jeans and jean jacket.
(Photo: Levi Strauss)

Glossary of Textile Terms

Acetate. A synthetic fiber processed from wood pulp. If you have a jacket made of acetate, you're wearing a "lumber" jacket. Acetate has luxurious feel and appearance and a wide range of colors; it is relatively fast-drying and economical.

Acrylic. Name for a manufactured synthetic fiber derived from coal, air, water, petroleum, and limestone. Wear an acrylic fur coat to stay warm and save a beaver. Acrylic fabrics are soft, warm, and lightweight; an acrylic fabric's shape is retentive, and it is quick-drying and resistant to sunlight, weather, oil, and chemicals.

Bias. Much cloth is cut diagonally—known as bias cutting—in order to make clothes fit smoother and wear better. Sometimes it's good to go against the grain.

Blend. A term to describe a yarn composed of two or more types of fiber—such as polyester and cotton—to get the good characteristics of both. Lettuce with tomato is better than lettuce alone (if you like tomatoes).

Bonding. This term is used interchangeably to identify two different processes. One is the production of nonwoven fabric by combining fibers through the use of pressure, adhesives, and mechanical means. The other is the joining of two fabrics (like a jacket and its lining) using an adhesive rather than stitching.

Broadcloth. A popular variety of cloth, so named because it was
originally made on a wide loom. The term today has no special significance. It usually refers to a fine, closely woven,
lustrous cotton or polyester/cotton fabric made in plain weave
with a fine rib in the direction of the filling.

Canvas. A family of strong, firm, closely woven fabrics, made of
cotton or synthetic fiber. Basic uses include tents and awn-
ings.

Cellulose. The basic substance of all vegetable fibers and some
synthetic fibers. Squash and cook a spruce tree down to a
sticky liquid and you have cellulose. This can then be made
into fiber that can be turned into cloth. Many Americans
"spruce up" daily in clothes made of cellulose fiber.

Chambray. This lightweight cotton fabric can look a lot like
denim, but it isn't. It looks that way because the thread that
goes one way in the weave is dyed and the one that goes the
other way is white. People wear chambray shirts who can't
even pronounce chambray (SHAM-bray).

Corduroy. From the French *corde du roi*, meaning "King's cord."
This popular cut pile fabric, usually cotton, with the familiar
raised ribs is nearly as common as denim. The rib effect is
caused by fibers extending from the cloth surface. Corduroy
trousers are easily identified by that "zip-zip" sound as the
wearer walks.

Denim. A sturdy, economical cotton twill cloth, usually blue,
although it can be done in any color. Fifty million cowboys
can't be wrong. Variations include checks, patterns, and
stripes.

Doeskin. A soft, high-quality, smooth, slightly napped woolen
fabric that looks in some ways like buckskin. It's used for
fine garments—and the tops of fine pool tables.

Double-knit. A knit fabric with a double stitch to give double
thickness to the cloth. In double-knits, both sides of the
fabric look similar. It makes a neat knit fit.

Duck. Another name for canvas, one of the world's most durable
fabrics, made in many weights. Made into sails, duck naturally takes to water.

Durable press. A finish achieved with the use of resins and heat
curing that enables a garment to keep its shape after washing
with little or no ironing. Life has enough wrinkles, try durable press.

Elasticity. The ability of a fabric to stretch, then pop back to its original shape. And fabric doesn't have to diet to do it.

Fabric weight. The number of ounces a particular fabric weighs per yard. The lighter the weight, usually the cooler the cloth.

Felt. Felt material is made by bonding fibers together through the use of heat, moisture, and pressure, rather than through weaving or knitting. Fine hats are usually felt.

Flame-retardant. Term used to describe fabrics that have received a chemical treatment to make them resist burning. The U.S. textile industry is spending millions of dollars each year to develop flame-retardant fabrics.

Flocking. The application of short fibers to fabric or other material by the use of adhesives or an electrostatic machine to give a plush, velvet, or suede effect. Also used to put dots or figures on sheer fabrics like curtains.

Gabardine. A tough, hard-finished twill fabric made of cotton, wool, or blended yarn that is known for its long wear. You can wear gabardine anywhere, but you can't wear it out.

Gingham. A cotton fabric with threads dyed in different colors to create a simple plaid or check design often associated with tablecloths. Also made in stripes. Ginghams with two colors are generally called *checks*; three colors or more, *plaids*. You can take gingham out of the country, but you can't take the country out of gingham.

Gray goods (greige). Gray goods are raw fabrics straight from the loom without being bleached, dyed, or finished.

Handwoven cloth. Cloth woven manually with an old-fashioned hand-and-foot loom. Handwoven goods are usually so durable that they become hand-me-downs.

Insulation. The ability of a fabric to trap air in its structure between fibers, forming a buffer against excessive cold or heat. When you buy a good insulating cloth, the air comes free.

Interfacing. A cloth or padding that is put between the outside and the inside lining of a piece of clothing to help the garment hold its shape or to add warmth. Sometimes called *interlining*.

Jacquard. A weaving process, named after its inventor, that permits the automatic insertion of intricate designs into the fabric, including raised patterns. Some examples: drapery and upholstery fabric, bath towels, bedspreads. Thanks to

Jacquard there are dresses with figures on them as good as the figures in them.

Jean. A rugged, close-woven cotton or blended twill fabric that is very popular for sportswear and work clothes. Sometimes used interchangeably with *denim*. Jean's first name, incidentally, is not "blue."

Lisle fabric. A finely knit cloth of silky appearance made from the best and longest cotton fibers. It makes fine underwear, silken T-shirts, and hosiery.

Madras. A lightweight (usually cotton) fabric with stripes, cords, or checks that is guaranteed to "bleed" or fade with wear. They say that good Madras never dyes, it just fades away. Gets its name from the Madras section of India where it originated and is still made.

Modacrylic. Generic term for synthetic fiber made from elements obtained from natural gas, coal, air, salt, and water. Soft, resilient, abrasive, and flame-resistant. Major uses include deep-pile coats, fake fur, wigs, nonwoven fabrics, blankets, and carpets.

Muslin. One of the oldest known plain weave fabrics. The muslin family is popular for bedsheets, shirts, pajamas, dress fabrics, furniture coverings, lamp shades, and much more. Your head on a pillow could be nuzzlin' muslin, but the odds are, it's now a polyester/cotton blend instead of all-cotton as in the past.

Napping. A process of making a fabric fuzzy by passing it over brushes to give it a more pleasing appearance or to make it warmer to the touch. Just a smooth way of putting up a good front.

Nonwoven. A sheet of material made without the usual knitting or weaving process, using heat, pressure, chemicals, adhesives, needle-punch, or sewing to bind the fibers together. Check your rug's mat or an old felt hat—that's where it's at.

Nylon. Generic name for the first fiber made entirely from chemicals. Basic raw materials are petroleum or natural gas, air, and water. Known for strength, elasticity, and wear resistance. Lustrous, easy to wash, and resistant to many chemicals. Major uses include hosiery and apparel, bedspreads, carpets and draperies, ropes and nets, tarpaulins, tents, and tire cords.

Oxford. A soft, easily laundered fabric made from cotton or rayon with a modified plain or basket weave. It's one of four shirt cloths originally made in England and named after famous universities, so it must be pretty smart. If it's a button-down shirt, chances are it's oxford cloth.

Percale. A long-wearing, tightly woven cotton with a fine texture, highly favored in the making of bedsheets. Differs from muslin in that there are more threads to the square inch. So, for smooth bedding, avail yourself of percale.

Pile. The raised loops, tufts, or knots that form all or a part of the surface of some fabrics—for example, shag carpet.

Polyester. Generic name for the most-used synthetic fiber. Blended with cotton and other fiber, or used alone, polyester is a basic ingredient of most durable press fabrics. A strong, shrink-resistant fiber, quick-drying and resistant to wrinkles. Widely used in apparel and home furnishings of all kinds.

Poplin. A tightly woven, heavyweight broadcloth used in both dress and casual clothes and in uniforms.

Preshrunk. Clothes or material that have been shrunk deliberately before sale to remove the tendency of the fabric to shrink when washed or laundered. It may still shrink a little, but not from maxi to mini at a hint of rain.

Quilting. Two pieces of fabric with padding in between, held in place by stitching. This form of insulation makes good ski clothes—and cushions the falls.

Rayon. First of the synthetic fibers available in the U.S. and for many years the only one. Originally made from cotton waste, but now made from wood pulp. A versatile and economical fiber known for its high absorbency, softness, and comfort. So remember, the log that gave you splinters yesterday may be your smooth silky shirt tomorrow.

Reprocessed wool. Wool that has been reclaimed from scraps of cloth never used by consumers, as opposed to "virgin" wool, which is taken directly from new-cut fleece. The difference could be so small you couldn't tell it unless the wool were pulled over your eyes.

Seconds. Yarns, fabrics, or finished garments that fail to meet the manufacturer's standards for quality and must be sold at lower prices. Because some of the imperfections are so minor, many seconds are a first-class value.

Seersucker. A light, crinkled, usually striped cloth made of cotton or synthetic fiber that is excellent for cool summer use and needs no ironing. When you think stripes, you have to think of tigers, barber poles, peppermint candy, and seersucker suits.

Selvage. The tighter-woven edge on either side of some fabrics, usually reinforced in some manner to keep it from raveling. Keeps the cloth edges straight so you'll get the straight goods.

Serge. Rhymes with "urge." A formal, dressy type of wool twill fabric that comes in a variety of weights and becomes shiny with prolonged use. It's okay for your shoes to shine, but not your pants—but nobody knows why.

Sharkskin. Any of a number of high-grade, worsted, twill fabrics of lightweight, smooth finish and high durability that remotely resemble the rough hide of a shark. You wouldn't want a live shark's skin to get too close to your skin.

Shrinkage. Reduction in length and/or width of fabric, usually because of washing. This could make a size 18 into a size 8 after a rainstorm without modern textile technology.

Silk. A fine, strong, smooth fabric made of threadlike fibers produced by caterpillars that feed entirely on mulberry leaves. When you say something is silky, you mean super smooth, super nice, and just plain super.

Sizing. When you add starch or similar materials to fabrics to add strength, body, weight, smoothness, or stiffness, that's sizing. Also applied to yarn to give strength and prevent damage in weaving. In a finishing process, a little size makes a big difference.

Skein. In plain language, a ball of yarn. Technically, a strand of yarn or thread of any desired length wound onto a coil or reel.

Suede cloth. Woven or knit fabrics, made with a soft, fuzzy surface to resemble suede leather. Recent textile technology has given some suede cloth an appearance and ease of care superior to real suede. So, switch to suede—cloth, that is.

Terry cloth. A soft fabric—usually cotton—with a rough surface composed of uncut yarn loops, highly favored in the making of towels and bathrobes. Loops sometimes sheared to produce velvet effect. A very drying subject.

Textiles. In its broadest sense, *textiles* refers to fabrics of any

and all kinds regardless of how they are made or what they are made from. From surgical gauze to circus tents. From tire cord to rocket nose cones.

Thermal knit. A lightweight fabric, usually used for special, cold-weather underwear. Traps air in a large, open honeycomb weave to keep the wearer warm in icy weather. The original hotpants.

Trade names. Names given certain products by manufacturers to distinguish them from competing brands that are similar. Dacron, Kodel, and Fortrel are all trade names for polyester fiber.

Tricot. A thin, knit fabric made with two sets of threads that has fine, riblike lines running from top to bottom on one side, crosswise on the other side. Used extensively for lingerie and women's nightwear. Most people do not pronounce the last letter of tricot: pronounce it "TREE-coh."

Tweed. A rough-finished family of fabrics, often handwoven, of legendary toughness and long wear. Usually recognizable by its hairy surface and coarse look. Made in a variety of colors, designs, and constructions. Wearing out a tweed suit is about as hard as throwing away a boomerang.

Velour. Any of a number of woven or knitted materials with a soft, smooth appearance resembling velvet. There is allure in soft velour.

Virgin wool. A legal term used to indicate use of a wool that has never before been made into yard or cloth, also called *new wool*. Mary had a little lamb, its fleece was virgin wool.